Fortress • 40

Ancient Greek Fortifications 500–300 BC

Nic Fields • Illustrated by Brian Delf

Series editors Marcus Cowper & Nikolai Bogdanovic

First published in 2006 by Osprey Publishing
Midland House, West Way, Botley, Oxford OX2 0PH, UK
443 Park Avenue South, New York, NY 10016, USA
E-mail: info@ospreypublishing.com

ISBN 1 84176 884 7

Design: Ken Vail Graphic Design, Cambridge, UK
Cartography: Map Studio Ltd, Romsey, UK
Index by Alison Worthington
Originated by PPS-Grasmere, Leeds, UK
Printed in China through Bookbuilders

06 07 08 09 10   10 9 8 7 6 5 4 3 2 1

A CIP catalogue record for this book is available from the British Library.

FOR A CATALOGUE OF ALL BOOKS PUBLISHED BY OSPREY MILITARY AND AVIATION
PLEASE CONTACT:

NORTH AMERICA
Osprey Direct, C/o Random House Distribution Center, 400 Hahn Road, Westminster,
MD 21157
E-mail: info@ospreydirect.com

ALL OTHER REGIONS
Osprey Direct UK, P.O. Box 140, Wellingborough, Northants, NN8 2FA, UK
E-mail: info@ospreydirect.co.uk

www.ospreypublishing.com

Artist's note

Editor's note

When classical authors are referred to throughout the text the
standard form of reference has been adopted. The formula used is
'author', 'title' (if the author wrote more than one work) followed
by a one-, two- or three-figure reference. If the work is a play or
poem, the figure reference indicates either 'line', or 'book' and
'line'. Thus 'Homer (*Odyssey* 8.512)' refers to line 512 of the eighth
book of the *Odyssey*. Alternatively, if the work is a treatise, the
figure reference indicates 'book' and 'chapter', or 'book', 'chapter'
and 'paragraph'. Thus 'Strabo (13.1.32)' refers to paragraph 32 of
the first chapter of the 13th book of the only surviving work by
Strabo. When modern authors are referred to throughout the
text the Harvard system of referencing has been adopted. The
formula used is 'author', 'publication date' followed by page
number(s). Thus 'Drews (1993: 106)' refers to page 106 of his
1993 publication, that is, *The end of the Bronze Age: Changes in
Warfare and the Catastrophe c.1200 BC*.

Abbreviations

FGrHist	F. Jacoby, *Die Fragmente der griechischen Historiker* (Berlin & Leiden, 1923–)
Fornara	C. W. Fornara, *Translated Documents of Greece and Rome I: Archaic Times to the end of the Peloponnesian War* (Cambridge, 1983)
Harding	P. Harding, *Translated Documents of Greece and Rome 2: From the end of the Peloponnesian War to the battle of Ipsus* (Cambridge, 1985)
IG	*Inscriptiones Graecae* (Berlin, 1923–)
Maier I	F. G. Maier, *Griechische Mauerbauinschrifen I* (Heidelberg, 1959)
Maier II	F. G. Maier, *Griechische Mauerbauinschrifen II* (Heidelberg, 1961)
Tod	M. N. Tod, *A Selection of Greek Historical Inscriptions vol. 2: 403 BC to 323 BC* (Oxford, 1948)

The Fortress Study Group (FSG)

The object of the FSG is to advance the education of the public in
the study of all aspects of fortifications and their armaments,
especially works constructed to mount or resist artillery. The FSG
holds an annual conference in September over a long weekend
with visits and evening lectures, an annual tour abroad lasting
about eight days, and an annual Members' Day.
The FSG journal FORT is published annually, and its newsletter
Casemate is published three times a year. Membership is
international. For further details, please contact:

The Secretary, c/o 6 Lanark Place, London W9 1BS, UK

The Coast Defenses Study Group (CDSG)

The Coast Defense Study Group (CDSG) is a non-profit
corporation formed to promote the study of coast defenses and
fortifications, primarily but not exclusively those of the United
States of America; their history, architecture, technology, and
strategic and tactical employment. Membership in the CDSG
includes four issues of the organization's two quarterly
publications the Coast Defense Journal and the CDSG
Newsletter. For more information about the CDSG please visit
www.cdsg.org, or to join the CDSG write to:

The Coast Defense Study Group, Inc., 634 Silver Dawn Court,
Zionsville, IN 46077-9088 (Attn: Glen Williford)

Contents

Introduction

For the Greeks the characteristic form of political organization was that of the city-state (*polis*), the small autonomous community, with publicly funded institutions, confined to one city and its hinterland. It was, as Aristotle so neatly expressed it, 'an association of several villages that achieves almost complete self-sufficiency' (*Politics* 1252b8). No 'city' in the modern sense was created, for the association established a new and overriding citizenship in which the political independence of the ancestral villages was submerged forever. For Aristotle man was 'by nature an animal of the *polis*' (*Politics* 1253a9), being designed by his nature to realize his full potential through living the good life within the framework of the *polis*, the key signifier of civilization. Appropriately, Aristotle (*Politics* 1275a5–8) defined the citizen (*politai*) as the man who shares in political judgement and rule.

As an agrarian-based society, the *polis* controlled and exploited a territory (*chōra*), which was delimited geographically by mountains or sea, or by proximity to another *polis*. The nearest and most powerful neighbour was the natural enemy. Border wars were thus common, as were inter-*polis* agreements and attempts to establish territorial rights over disputed areas. Autonomy was jealously guarded, but the necessities of collaboration made for a proliferation of foreign alliances, leagues of small communities, usually ethnically related, and hegemonies. There was also constant interchange and competition between *poleis*, so that despite their separate identities a common culture was always maintained.

While the *polis* was defined in terms of its citizens (e.g. the Athenians not Athens) rather than geographically or through bricks and marble, its development was also a process of urbanization and the walled city, for instance, is common in Homer. Undeniably the archaeological remains of Bronze Age Greece reveal fortifications of great strength and complexity, as at Mycenae, Tiryns and Gla, yet these Mycenaean citadels are the counterparts of medieval castles rather than of walled cities. But when the residential fortress ceases to be the citadel and becomes the city, fortifications now protect the citizen body and not merely the ruler and his household. Greek *poleis*, to quote Winter, 'were much more than fortresses, they were complete social, political and economic units to a degree never achieved by their modern successors' (1971: xvi).

Raised and maintained by the state, the circuit, usually of sun-dried mud-brick resting on a low rubble socle, was not very high or very strong. For it did not yet need to be as *polis* conflict was decided by spear and shield, though some attempt was made to give protection to city gateways. In Anatolia, amongst the East Greeks, stronger fortifications are well attested by the results of excavation, though at the turn of the 5th century BC these could not defeat the siegecraft that the Persians had learned from the Assyrians. But in Greece proper, city walls, simple as they were, sufficed for their purpose, and would remain so until the technology of attack (mechanics) had caught up with that of defence (construction) through the invention of the torsion-spring catapult (*katapéltes*, 'shield-piercer') by military engineers in the employ of Philip II of Macedon.

Chronology of major events

499–479 BC, PERSIAN WARS

499–494 BC Ionian Revolt

498 BC battle of Sepeia (Sparta triumphs over Argos); Athenians and Eretrians burn Sardis

498/497 BC Persians retake Cyprus (fall of Palaipaphos)

494 BC battle of Lade (fall of Miletos)

491 BC Dareios I demands 'earth and water' from Greeks; Gelon tyrant of Gela

490 BC Persians sack Naxos, Karystos, Eretria; battle of Marathon; accession of Leonidas

486 BC accession of Xerxes

483/482 BC Persians dig Athos canal; Themistokles' naval programme

480 BC Xerxes crosses Hellespont; battles of Thermopylai (Leonidas killed), Artemision, Salamis; Gelon defeats Carthaginians at Himera

479 BC battles of Plataia (Mardonios killed), Mykale

479–460 BC, EMERGENCE OF IMPERIAL ATHENS

479/478 BC Foundation of Delian League (anti-Persian)

478 BC City Walls of Athens begun; expeditions to Byzantium, Sestos, Cyprus; Sparta leaves Delian League

476/475 BC expeditions to Eion, Skyros (bones of 'Theseus')

474 BC Hieron of Syracuse defeats Etruscans at Kyme

467 BC fall of tyranny in Syracuse

c.466 BC Eurymedon campaign

465 BC Thasos quits Delian League

461/460 BC Athenian alliance with Argos, Thessaly, Megara

460–440 BC, FIRST PELOPONNESIAN WAR

460 BC Athenian expedition to Egypt

c.458 BC Long Walls of Athens begun

458 BC Saronic Gulf conflict (siege of Aigina); Athenian victories in Megarid

458/457 BC battles of Tanagra, Oenophyta (Athens controls Boiotia); Athenian alliance with Egesta

454 BC disaster for Athens in Nile Delta

454/453 BC Delian League treasury transferred from Delos to Athens (metamorphosis of league to empire complete)

453 BC revolts of Erythrai, Miletos; first extant Athenian Tribute List

451 BC five-year truce between Athens and Sparta, Kimon campaigns (and dies) on Cyprus

449/448 BC Peace of Kallias (détente between Athens and Persia)

447/446 BC revolts in Boiotia, Euboia; battle of First Koroneia (ends Athens' control of Boiotia), secession of Megara

446 BC Spartan invasion of Attica; Perikles quashes Euboian revolt

446/445 BC Thirty Years Peace

440 BC Samos rebels

440–432 BC, BETWEEN THE WARS

439 BC Samos surrenders

c.435 BC Perikles' Black Sea expedition

434 BC Corcyra and Corinth clash

433 BC Athenian alliance with Corcyra; battle of Sybota

433/432 BC Athenian alliances with Leontini, Rhegion

432 BC Potidaia rebels; conferences at Sparta and ultimatum to Athens

432–421 BC, PELOPONNESIAN WAR (Archidamian War)

431 BC Thebes attacks Plataia; Sparta's first invasion of Attica

430 BC Potidaia surrenders

429 BC Phormio's naval victories; plague in Athens (Perikles dies)

429/427 BC siege of Plataia

428/427 BC Mytilene rebels

426 BC Sparta sends colony to Herakleia Trachinia; Demosthenes' Aetolian campaign

425 BC Pylos campaign

424 BC battle of Delion; Brasidas' Thracian campaign

422 BC battle of Amphipolis (Brasidas and Kleon killed)

421 BC Peace of Nikias

421–413 BC, PELOPONNESIAN WAR (Phoney Peace)

420 BC Alkibiades' quadruple alliance between Athens, Argos, Mantineia, Elis

418 BC battle of First Mantineia (opportunity to defeat Sparta on land squandered)

416 BC Athenians sack Melos (Thucydides' *Melian Dialogue*)

415 BC Athenian expedition to Sicily

414 BC Gylippos sent to Syracuse; second expedition under Demosthenes

413 BC loss of Athenian armada at Syracuse

413–404 BC, PELOPONNESIAN WAR (Ionian War)

413 BC Spartans seize Dekeleia in Attica (*epiteichismos*)

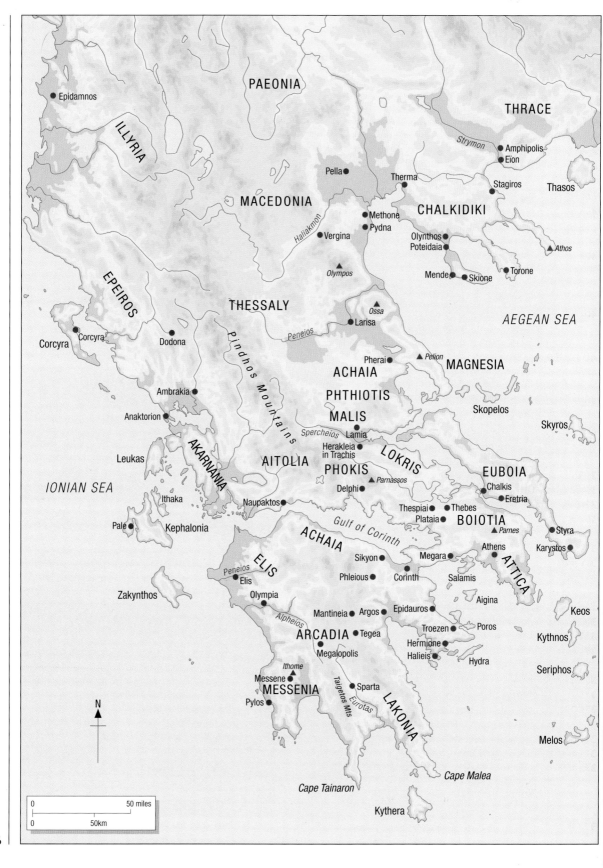

PAEONIA

THRACE

Epidamnos

ILLYRIA

Strymon

Amphipolis
Eion

Pella

Therma

Stagiros

Thasos

MACEDONIA

Haliakmon

Methone
Pydna

CHALKIDIKI

Olynthos
Poteidaia

▲ *Athos*

Vergina

Mende
Skione

Torone

▲ *Olympos*

THESSALY

EPEIROS

▲ *Ossa*

AEGEAN SEA

Corcyra

Dodona

Peneios

Larisa

Corcyra

Pindhos Mountains

Pherai

▲ *Pelion*

MAGNESIA

ACHAIA

PHTHIOTIS

Skopelos

Ambrakia

MALIS

Spercheios

Lamia

Skyros

Anaktorion

Herakleia
in Trachis

LOKRIS

AKARNANIA

AITOLIA

PHOKIS

EUBOIA

Leukas

▲ *Parnassos*

Chalkis

IONIAN SEA

Delphi

Eretria

Ithaka

Naupaktos

Thespiai ● ● Thebes

BOIOTIA

Styra

Pale

Kephalonia

Plataia

ACHAIA

Gulf of Corinth

▲ *Parnes*

Karystos

Athens

ATTICA

ELIS

Sikyon

Megara

Zakynthos

Peneios

Elis

Phleious

Corinth

Salamis

Olympia

Aigina

Keos

Alpheios

Mantineia

Argos

Epidauros

ARCADIA

Tegea

Troezen

Poros

Kythnos

Megalopolis

Hermione

Halieis

Hydra

Seriphos

▲ *Ithome*

Messene

Sparta

Taigetos Mts

Eurotas

MESSENIA

LAKONIA

Pylos

N

Melos

Cape Malea

Cape Tainaron

Kythera

0		50 miles
0		50km

412 BC	Spartan alliance with Persia and intervention in Aegean
411 BC	Four Hundred rule Athens (democracy overthrown); Euboia rebels; fleet at Samos under Thrasyboulos remains loyal to democracy (Alkibiades takes command); battles of Kynossema, Abydos
410 BC	battle of Kyzikos; democracy restored in Athens
409 BC	Spartans capture Chios
409/408 BC	Spartans retake Pylos
408 BC	Athenians capture Byzantium; Carthaginians sack Himera
408/407 BC	failed *coup d'état* of Hermokrates and Dionysios
406 BC	Carthaginians besiege Akragas; battle of Notion (Alkibiades' second downfall – flees to Thrace); battle of Arginousai (trial of Athenian *stratēgoi*)
405 BC	Akragas sacked; siege of Gela; Dionysios takes power in Syracuse as *stratēgos autokrator* (treaty with Carthage); accession of Artaxerxes II Mnemon; battle of Aigospotami
404 BC	Alkibiades assassinated; Athens defeated (swears oath to follow Sparta 'by land and sea')

404–386 BC, SPARTAN HEGEMONY

404/403 BC	Thirty Tyrants rule Athens (Spartan garrison on Acropolis)
403 BC	Thrasyboulos captures Peiraieus (democracy restored)
401 BC	rebellion of Kyros the younger; battle of Cunaxa (march of Ten Thousand – Xenophon's *Anabasis*)
398 BC	Persia builds fleet for Athens (Admiral Konon)
398/397 BC	Dionysios I besieges Motya
396 BC	battle of Sardis
394 BC	battles of Nemea River, Second Koroneia, Knidos
391 BC	rebellion of Evagoras of Salamis
390 BC	Iphikrates defeats Spartan *mora* at Lechaion
387 BC	Dionysios I captures Rhegion

386–371 BC, DEFEAT OF SPARTA

385 BC	Agesipolis captures Mantineia
382 BC	Phoebidas captures Kadmeia
379 BC	Spartans punish Phleious, capture Olynthos (apogee of Sparta's power)
379/378 BC	Kadmeia liberated (Thebes new 'superpower')
378 BC	Sphodrias raids Attica
378/377 BC	Thebans 'liberate' Thespiai; foundations of Boiotian League; Second Athenian Confederation
377 BC	Agesilaos invades Boiotia
376 BC	Peloponnesian fleet defeated off Naxos
375 BC	Iason of Pherai elected *tagos* of Thessaly; Timotheos' expedition to Corcyra (victory off Alizeia); Sacred Band (under Pelopidas) defeat Spartans at Tegyra
371 BC	Athens and Sparta become allies, but Spartans defeated at Leuktra by Epameinondas

371–360 BC, THEBAN HEGEMONY

370/369 BC	Epameinondas' first invasion of Peloponnese, (Messenia liberated, Mantineia re-founded)
369 BC	Epameinondas' second invasion (reduces Sparta's effective allies to Corinth, Phleious)
367 BC	Dionysios I sends second force of mercenaries; Sparta wins 'Tearless Battle' against Arcadians; death of Dionysios I (son succeeds as Dionysios II)
367/366 BC	Satraps' Revolt
366/365 BC	Epameinondas' third invasion of Peloponnese (final collapse of Peloponnese League)
365 BC	Pelopidas killed
364 BC	Thebes destroys Orchomenos
362 BC	Epameinondas' last invasion of Peloponnese, battle of Second Mantineia (Epameinondas killed)

360–336 BC, RISE OF MACEDON

360/359 BC	Accession of Philip II of Macedon
357–355 BC	Social War (ends Second Athenian Confederacy)
357 BC	Euboia revolts from Thebes; Philip captures Amphipolis, marries Olympias of Molossia
354 BC	Philip captures Methone (loses eye); Dion assassinated
353–346 BC	Sacred War (shatters Thebes)
352 BC	Philip's victory at 'Crocus Field'
348 BC	Philip captures Olynthos
346 BC	Peace of Philokrates (détente between Philip and Athens)
344 BC	Philip campaigns in Thrace, Epeiros, Thessaly (elected *tagos* for life); Dionysios II overthrown (retires to Corinth); Timoleon of Corinth arrives in Sicily
343 BC	Carthaginians capture Syracuse
342/341 BC	Philip and Athens clash in Chersonesos
341 BC	Timoleon defeats Carthaginians at Krimisos (reconstructs Sicily as *autokrator*); Athens intervenes on Euboia
340 BC	Alexander regent in Macedon, Philip besieges Perinthos, Byzantium, seizes Athenian grain-ships; Athens abrogates Peace of Philokrates
339 BC	Philip bypasses Thermopylai (garrisons Elateia); Athenian alliance with Thebes
338 BC	battle of Chaironeia
337 BC	League of Corinth (Philip proclaimed *hēgēmon* of Greeks); Lykourgos comes to prominence at Athens
336 BC	Philip assassinated (army acclaims Alexander III)

336–323 BC, ALEXANDER III 'THE GREAT'

336 BC	Alexander *hēgēmon* of Greeks
335 BC	campaigns in Thrace, Illyria, sack of Thebes
334 BC	Antipater regent of Macedon, Alexander crosses Hellespont (visits Troy), battle of Granikos; sieges of Miletos, Halikarnassos

333 BC	Gordian knot; Alexander defeats Dareios III at Issos; Dareios' first-peace offer
332 BC	submissions of Byblos, Sidon; sieges of Tyre, Gaza; Alexander crowned Pharaoh
331 BC	visit to Siwah; foundation of Alexandria; Dareios' final peace-offer; Alexander defeats Dareios at Gaugamela; Alexander enters Babylon
330 BC	destruction of Persepolis; Dareios murdered, Bessos (satrap of Bactria) proclaims himself 'Great King'
329 BC	Hindu Kush crossed; Bessos captured
328 BC	campaigns against Spitamenes (Bactria, Sogdia)
327 BC	Sogdian Rock captured
326 BC	Swat valley campaign; Alexander defeats Poros at Hydapses; mutiny at Hyphasis, siege of Multan (Alexander wounded)
325 BC	Alexander crosses Gedrosia; Nearchos sails to Persian Gulf
323 BC	Alexander dies in Babylon

323–301 BC, WARS OF THE SUCCESSORS

323 BC	Krateros, Perdikkas, Ptolemy, Seleukos et al. divide empire into rival spheres of power
323–322 BC	Greek mercenaries revolt (Bactria); Lamian War
317/316 BC	Kassandros (Antipater's son) holds Macedon (Demetrios of Phaleron puppet-ruler in Athens); foundations of Kassandreia, Thessalonika
316 BC	Antigonos' victory at Gabiene (Eumenes executed); Antigonos acclaimed 'King of all Asia'
312 BC	Ptolemy and Seleukos defeat Demetrios Poliorketes (Antigonos' son) at Gaza; Seleukos returns to Babylon
307 BC	Demetrios 'liberates' Athens (Demetrios of Phaleron exiled)
305–304 BC	Demetrios' fruitless siege of Rhodes
304 BC	Kassandros besieges Athens
303/302 BC	Agathokles invades southern Italy
301 BC	coalition of Ptolemy, Seleukos, Lysimachos against Antigonids; battle of Ipsos (Antigonos killed)

Individual sun-dried mud-bricks, which rest on a socle of rubble masonry, are clearly discernible in the West Gate of Eretria. As for the Athenians, the standard measurement employed by the Eretrians was the 'short foot'. (Author's collection)

Building methods

By combining the examination of the structures with the study of the documents and other written sources relating to their building we can begin to know something of the cost of Greek fortifications in terms of money, labour, materials and time. The study of the relevant literature also has the immediate value of enabling surviving fortifications in many cases to be dated with more precision than is possible by archaeological evidence alone.

Financing and labour

Military architecture, like religious or secular architecture, was financed with public funds or the spoils of a successful military campaign (Maier II.55–66, cf. Plutarch *Kimon* 13.6). Many affluent citizens too are known to have contributed money from their own capital. Konon the younger, albeit under compulsion, provided 10 talents from his own estate to repair the city walls of Athens (Nepos *Timotheos* 4.1). When the Athenians learned of the disastrous outcome of Chaironeia (338 BC), they straightway took steps to defend Athens against the Macedonians. The statesman Lykourgos gives a vivid account (*Against Leokrates* 44) of the measures undertaken at that moment:

> Men of every age offered their services for the city's defence on that occasion when the land was giving up its trees, the dead their gravestones, and the temple arms. Some set themselves to building walls, other to making ditches and palisades. Not a man in the city was idle.

The lower part of this domestic building in Argos is a socle of rubble masonry, with the upper parts built in sun-dried mud-brick. Albeit more substantial, many fortification walls had a superstructure largely of mud-brick. (Author's collection)

The orator Demosthenes boasts (18.118, cf. 248, 299–300) that he himself served as one of the wall builders (*teichopoioí*), spending 10 talents of public money (Aischines 3.23, cf. 31) and a further 100 *minae*, or 10,000 Attic drachmas, from his own estate (Aischines 3.17, Plutarch *Moralia* 845F, cf. 851A, Demosthenes 18.118) to repair his assigned section. Both in the Peloponnesian War (Thucydides 3.17.4) and in the time of Alexander the Great (*IG* ii^2 329.10 = Harding 102), a drachma was the daily pay of a soldier, thus giving a very rough idea of the value of a *mina*.

Once the decision to build, or repair, fortifications had been made the labour force, which included salaried professionals such as carpenters and stonemasons (Xenophon *Hellenika* 4.8.10), was assembled. It would be headed by an architect (*architékton*), the chief builder responsible both for the design and for the supervision of actual construction (Plato *Politikos* 259e–260a). When further work on the walls of Athens was undertaken in 307/306 BC an architect was elected by the assembly (*IG* ii^2 463.6–7, cf. 9). An earlier Athenian document, dating to 409/408 BC and recording the payments made to bring the Erechtheion to completion, records that an architect then received the standard day-wage rate of one Attic drachma (*IG* i^3 476, 60–61, 266–268). Another Athenian document, dating to 395/394 BC and recording sums disbursed for the rebuilding of the city walls, records daily payments of 160 Attic drachmas 'for the teams bringing the blocks' (Tod 107).

Planning

Architects preferred, when tracing out city walls, to try to make use of natural defences such as a precipitous hill. Thus the nucleus of many older cities was the acropolis, a hill that was defensible without being too high and inaccessible. Yet the acropolis could not be too far removed from the arable land it was meant to control. As Aristotle emphasizes (*Politics* 1330b2–3):

> The site of the city should likewise be convenient both for political administration and for war. With view to the latter it should afford easy egress to the citizens, but difficult to approach or blockade for any enemies.

Thus the ideal site was the tip of a spur, which ran out from the flank of a mountain and was linked to the main mass by a narrow ridge.

However, as circuits did not become common till the 6th century BC, or normal till the 5th century BC, walls tended to be loosely flung round the whole city at a comparatively late stage of its development, that is, when urban growth was in some sense complete. As Wycherley says, a circuit 'was not the frame into which the rest fitted' (1976: 39) and some cities would remain un-walled in the classical period, Sparta and Elis for example. Also, the military value of the acropolis decreased and would gradually disappear as an essential feature in the plan of a 5th- and 4th-century city. Hence Aristotle (*Politics* 1330b5) discusses the acropolis from the political rather than the military view point.

Building materials

Materials employed in Greek fortifications may be divided into two main groups: sun-dried mud-brick on a stone socle, and walls built entirely of stone.

Completion in mud-brick unquestionably saved a great deal of time and money. The bricks could be made rapidly with little apparatus and by unskilled labour. Nor were speed and cheapness the only advantages brick offered. Mud-brick is fireproof and practically indestructible to the weather when the surface is properly protected. Also, a brick construction is not affected by minor earthquake shocks. Demosthenes speaks (3.25–26, 23.207, cf. 13.29) of the brick houses of Themistokles, Miltiades and Aristides as still inhabited in his day, nearly 150 years later; indeed they were evidently in good condition and quite indistinguishable from their neighbours.

Yet there were comparatively few sites where bricks could be made in sufficient quantities. The process required a copious water supply as well as a vast amount of clay of a type that would not crumble or crack in a wall. Also, the manufacture of brick when limestone was around in abundance made the latter a more viable proposition. As a rule in Greece the ground was both encumbered with fragments of convenient size and interrupted by bare escarpments and outcrops – architects missed no opportunity for including stretches of bedrock in a wall – often so layered and cross-fissured that semi-rectangular blocks could be detached by means of wedges and crowbars alone. Under these conditions, if stone was left untrimmed, it could be gathered and put together in less time than would be spent in making and laying an equivalent number of bricks. Nevertheless, if a fortification was intended to be permanent, masons were employed at least to knock off the worse excrescences and, if financially possible, to dress some of the blocks. Yet, although all-stone fortifications became more common they never ousted mud-brick ones entirely.

Timber revetting reinforces this mud-brick wall in the village of Delphi. Ancient Greeks likewise employed timber to hold brickwork together, thereby preventing the structure from becoming weak as it attained height. (Author's collection)

The availability of materials and local prejudice continued to be the determining factors as to which construction was used. An Athenian inscription (*IG* ii² 463) of 307/306 BC deals, amongst other things, with repairs in brickwork to the pre-existing circuit of the same material, and Vitruvius (2.8.9) refers to the brickwork that existed in his day in the eastern and northern stretches of the city walls. At Olynthos abundant supplies of clay were available for domestic structures and fortification walls, whereas stone was evidently scarce. Similarly Mantineia, re-established by the Thebans, sat in an upland plain with an inexhaustible supply of clay, whereas its stone quarries were situated some distance away. The Mantineians, accordingly, rebuilt their city walls out of mud-brick.

Making bricks

An Eleusinian inscription of 329/328 BC hints that the clay for bricks required long preparation before it was put into wooden moulds, for there is no other way of explaining the very modest output of 125 bricks per day implied by the document's data. Still, with regards to financial matters the inscription is more informative. Clay to make 1,000 bricks cost four Attic drachmas, while the same number of bricks could be purchased ready made for 36 drachmas. Additionally, the daily wage for a skilled labourer was given as 2.5 Attic drachmas, while that of his assistant was 1.5 drachmas (*IG* ii² 1672, Maier I.20, 101).

Bricks were formed in wooden frames with a number of compartments. These were open at the top and bottom, which often resulted in a considerable difference in height of the bricks, while their length and width were regular. Several standard sizes and half-sizes were recognized, though each differs slightly from one locality to another. Nevertheless, the commonest sizes range from 0.4 to 0.5m, with a height of roughly 0.08m. The bricks that have been preserved in the fortifications at Corinth and Eleusis, for example, are almost identical in size (Corinthian bricks 0.45 × 0.45 × 0.09m, Eleusinian bricks 0.45 × 0.45 × 0.10m). According to the aforementioned Eleusinian document, bricks belonging to the Kimonian wall were 'one and one-half foot bricks' (*IG* ii² 1672.55–57, cf. Vitruvius 2.3.3), which suggests that the standard measurement employed at Eleusis and at Corinth was the 'short foot' (*c*.0.296m). Surviving bricks from Olynthos, on the other hand, are somewhat larger (0.49 × 0.49 × 0.09m). It appears, therefore, that Olynthos was using the 'long foot' (*c*.0.326m). Both units are probably of prehistoric origin.

If masonry replaced brick a wall could consist of random rubble, fieldstones found *in situ*, as is being speedily built here. However, rubble masonry could not provide the strength and size of wall required for military architecture. (Author's collection)

Quarrying stone

Masonry in dressed stone required the production of stone blocks to specified sizes, and these were quarried according to the specifications of the architect. As for bricks, measurements were given in half-foot (*hemipódion*) and foot (*poús*) lengths, subdivided into eight or 16 dactyls (fingers) respectively. The length and width of the block were measured out on the surface of the rock, and continuous channels were cut down vertically with hammer and chisel until the desired height was obtained. Notches were then chiselled under the bottom of the block, wooden wedges were inserted and soaked in water, and as the wedges expanded they broke the block free from its bed.

When quarried, a block was always several centimetres larger all round than the finished piece, the extra stone serving as a protective surface during transportation. Here the Greeks normally employed four-wheeled wagons drawn by oxen (Diodoros 4.18, *IG* ii 2² 1656.8, 1673.47, 66), although sledges and rollers were certainly used sometimes (*IG* xi 2 203b.97). The pulling power of a pair of oxen was 25 talents or about half a ton (Xenophon *Cyropaedia* 6.1.54), hence special innovations were required to move blocks over 20 tons. These included great wooden wheels fitted around individual blocks, which were then pulled along by teams of draft animals (Vitruvius 10.2.11–12).

Masonry styles

The Greeks believed that utility and beauty were inseparable (Xenophon *Memorabilia* 4.6.9), and this almost casual combination of exquisiteness and usefulness we find in their polygonal, trapezoidal and ashlar masonry. Though austerely utilitarian, fortification walls could still often be counted among the city's architectural glories. Aristotle says (*Politics* 1331a11) that the whole circuit ought to be an ornament as well as a protection. It would be the first sight to impress a visitor, and it was meant to have a depressing effect on an approaching enemy.

Briefly, the masonry of any wall belongs to one of three main groups: un-hewn, roughly hewn, or carefully hewn and jointed. The distinction between the first two styles is at best one of degree, and both may be classed simply as rubble masonry. The third group, which invariably consisted of faces of finely jointed masonry enclosing a fill of earth and broken stones, may be subdivided as follows:

Masonry styles		
UNCOURSED MASONRY	**COURSED MASONRY**	
Polygonal blocks Curvilinear blocks (Scranton's 'Lesbian masonry') Trapezoidal blocks ('irregular trapezoidal') Ashlar blocks ('irregular ashlar')	Trapezoidal blocks Ashlar blocks	In both, courses may be all the same height (isodomic) or they may vary in height (pseudo-isodomic)

If masonry was to replace mud-brick fortifications, random rubble, broken stones collected in their natural condition, could not provide the strength and size of wall required. Stone specially trimmed and fitted was essential.

Trapezoidal masonry, which appears in the later part of the 5th century BC, was a compromise between ashlar and polygonal. Such blocks are flat on top and bottom, and equal in height throughout each course, but every now and then an end is cut on the slant, causing an overlap at the joint. Usually overlaps occur towards left and right alternately. Masonry of this kind looked civilized and was easy to build, yet interlocked enough for the builders to feel safe in using comparatively small blocks. Consequently the style was much used in military architecture, especially in the 100 years following its introduction.

Polygonal, because of its superior powers of cohesion, was never superseded for such purposes as fortifications, where large blocks could be found on the

spot in shapes easily trimmed to interlock. Polygonal masonry tended to consist of larger stones than coursed masonry, and the larger the stones the more stable the wall would be. First appearing in the early 6th century BC, mature polygonal work was distinguishable chiefly by the preponderance of projections at right angles or nearly right angles.

In all styles of carefully hewn and fitted masonry further distinctions may be made on the basis of the treatment of the faces and joints of the blocks. In general, architects preferred to give fortification walls an appearance of massive

ABOVE LEFT The north wall, Gyphtokastro, reveals the method of construction employed in military architecture. Stone specially quarried, trimmed and fitted was restricted to an outer and inner 'skin', the space between being filled with inferior material, broken stone, earth, and other material. (Author's collection)

ABOVE RIGHT A socle of polygonal masonry at Eleusis. Because of its superior powers of cohesion, the polygonal style was favoured for such purposes as fortification. Large blocks could be found *in situ* in shapes easily trimmed to interlock. (Author's collection)

Surface treatment

Quarry	Little, using pointed hammer, or no attempt made to finish block face
Hammer	Using pointed hammer, block face consciously roughened
Broached	In removing larger projections with punch, vertical furrows left on block face
Pointed	Block face brought to flat surface, but not smooth

and rugged strength, even when using a highly artificial technique.

The cutting and finishing of blocks was done with saws and drills, and, primarily, with hammers and chisels. Chisels were of iron and came in a variety of shapes and sizes. Their most common shapes were the point, the toothed or claw chisel, and the flat or drove chisel. If the rough, quarry surface was to be removed and the outer faces worked down, then this was achieved with a claw chisel first and then with a drove. The inner faces of the blocks, however, were left in the rough state in which they were quarried so as to help bind the fill of

13

In trapezoidal masonry, as here at Gyphtokastro, the horizontal joints between the blocks are for the most part parallel, but the vertical joints are skewed. Smaller chinking stones, often triangular, are sometimes used between the larger blocks. (Author's collection)

Ashlar masonry, east wall of Phyle. Rectangular in form, all the blocks are longer than they are tall, but the length may vary along the course. When the courses are uniform in height, as here, the stonework is isodomic. (Author's collection)

earth and rubble together. The top and bottom resting surfaces of the block were always dressed to a plane. The vertical joint surfaces were treated with *anathyrosis*, namely, only a narrow band along the vertical edges and top was finished smooth, while the rest of the surface was recessed slightly and left rough picked. As the Greeks laid their blocks absolutely dry, without bonding material, this treatment allowed a tight joint with a minimum of effort and expense since only the narrow strip of stone needed to make close contact with its neighbour.

Lifting stones

There were a variety of means for lifting blocks into place. Most commonly employed were lifting bosses (*ankones*), rectangular protrusions of the original protective envelope that were retained on opposite faces of the block when the rest of the surface was worked down. Such bosses, located at the centre of gravity, served as handles with either rope slings or iron tongs. Once the block was in place these bosses were removed in the final stages of construction.

As an alternative to lifting bosses, a deep U-shaped groove could be cut into each end of a block for lifting ropes. These could be easily pulled from the rope-grooves after placement. Another lifting device was the 'lewis bolt', a set of one flat and two wedge-shaped iron bars. These bars were set into a trapezoidal cutting on the top surface of the block and pinned together, the pin also passing through a stirrup-ring for attaching the hoisting rope (Heron *Mēchanika* 3.8). All cuttings for these various lifting devices were placed in such a way as to be hidden in the finished wall.

Workers lifted the block into place by means of a high tripod, windlasses, multiply pulleys and rope. Once in its proper course, the block was moved closer to its correct location on wooden rollers. Crowbars were needed for the final positioning; to give them purchase, shallow indentations, or pry-holes, were cut into the top of the course below.

Fortifications

The life of the *polis* was founded upon agriculture and remained dependent on it. This was recognized by Aristotle (*Politics* 1256a7) who contended that most citizens made their living by farming. The central task of fortifications, therefore, was the defence of the *polis'* territory (*chōra*) rather than its urban core (*astu*). This is not to deny the political and religious importance of the latter. However, given the limitations of tactics and ideology, territorial invasion could achieve the desired result by bringing about a single battle at a far lower cost than a direct assault, that is, in the type of warfare at which hoplites excelled on the kind of ground to which their arms and tactics were most suited. Further, practical considerations in the form of the expense of siege warfare also curtailed its use. These difficulties persisted into the early 4th century BC and are reflected in the slow development of Greek fortifications as compared with those of the Near East. Hence Greeks tended to rely on the circuit itself as a vertical barrier, punctuated by simple-opening gateways, whose primary purpose was to counter hoplite attack and not elaborate siege techniques.

Around 500 BC a major innovation, perhaps borrowed from Near-Eastern sources, appears with the addition of two-storeyed towers at vital points along the circuit to provide more convenient and numerous opportunities for flanking fire. These towers were rectangular in shape in accordance with eastern practice, with a covered chamber in the second storey and an open fighting platform protected by a parapet at roof level. Gateways were also better protected, being sheltered by a tower or towers, or by a deep inward jog, or by both these features to form entranceways of the forecourt type. Sprawling, contour-hugging fortifications (*Geländemauer* circuits) now began to encompass the whole built-up area of the city, though financial considerations often limited the extent of the circuit. This concept of defending the urban area replaced the concept of a defensible strongpoint like the acropolis.

Athens (Attica)

The city walls of Athens, with their thick stone socle and frequent use of towers, established a pattern that was to be copied in other fortifications of the period. Also Athens, which was capable of deploying the far larger resources necessary for the expensive business of defence, started the trend for a new form of fortification in the 'long wall'. Connecting a city to its port, such fortifications produced a new strategy associated with the name of Perikles. At the outbreak of the Peloponnesian War he persuades his fellow citizens to look upon the city of Athens, with its port, the Peiraieus now linked to it by the Long Walls, as an island, and not try to defend the *chōra* of Attica. At the same time, the fleet was to be used to maintain the empire (Thucydides 1.143.5, 2.13.2).

Perikles was a statesman deeply committed to a purely maritime empire. As war now threatened he expected his fellow citizens to simply man the walls and the fleet, and the rest of Attica would have to look after itself. Yet the majority of the Athenians, as Thucydides says (2.14.2), normally lived in the countryside, and Aristophanes in the *Acharnians* (32–33) and elsewhere (*Knights* 40–43, *Pax* 1320–1328, *Farmers* [Dindorf frs. 162, 163], *Islands* [Dindorf fr. 344]) gives vivid glimpses of the deep attachment of a large section of the population to the soil of Attica. So when Perikles takes the radical step of breaking the rules of agonal warfare by shifting the entire population behind the city walls, there are cries of anguish from the Attic countrymen since 'each of them felt as if he was leaving his native city' (Thucydides 2.16.2).

The Kerameikós, 'the most beautiful suburb of Athens' (Thucydides 2.34.5), is named after Keramos, the son of Dionysos and Ariadne (Pausanias 1.3.1). It is here that the best-preserved section of the City Wall, including the Dipylon Gate and Sacred Gate, stands. (Author's collection)

Epiteichismoi

During the Peloponnesian War an innovative use of seapower was the establishment of a permanent fortified base (*epiteichismos*, 'to-plant-a-fortification-in-enemy-territory') on or off the enemy's seaboard from which troops could damage, harass, and discourage and demoralize the enemy. Such bases were planted by the Athenians at Pylos (425 BC), a headland on the west coast of Messenia, and on Kythera (413 BC), the island just off the south-eastern tip of Lakonia (Thucydides 4.3–5, 7.26, cf. 4.53–54). The establishment of these Athenian strongholds within enemy territory did stir up trouble for the Spartans as they led to an increase in helot unrest. Yet such a scheme does not appear to be a component of the Periklean strategy, and the Corinthians first advocated the use of *epiteichismoi* in 432 BC (Thucydides 1.122.1). In truth Perikles only envisaged the use of *epiteichismoi* as a countermove if the Spartans attempted to establish a base in Attica (Thucydides 1.142.2–4), as they eventually did, on Alkibiades' recommendation, at Dekeleia on Mount Parnes (413 BC). Visible from Athens itself, this 'fort was built to threaten and control the plain and the richest parts of the *chōra*' (Thucydides 7.19.2). The position was well chosen. For, in contrast to their annual ineffective invasions of Attica (431 BC, 430 BC, 428 BC, 427 BC and 425 BC), the raids made by the Spartans and their allies were now unremitting. Occupied year-round, Dekeleia became the *epiteichismos* par excellence (Andokides 1.101, Lysias 14.30, Isokrates 16.10, *Hellenika Oxyrhynchia* 12.3).

Topography

Ancient Athens consisted of the city itself and Attica, the large triangular peninsula jutting southward into the Aegean Sea. The city sat on a large coastal plain in north-west Attica, surrounded by four mountains (Aigaleos, Parnes, Pentele, Hymettos). Running through the plain in a north-east to south-west orientation is a long limestone ridge. Near its south-western end, this ridge comprises the Acropolis, the Mouseion (Philopappos Hill) and the Hill of the Nymphs, with the Pnyx, the meeting place of the Athenian assembly, lying in between.

The classical city developed around the Acropolis, which now served as the centre for civic and cultic activity. Beyond its slopes, a circuit, running some 6.5km in circumference, enclosed the urban area. The latter Thucydides tells us (2.15.3–4), shrewdly using the evidence of public monuments, was on the south side of the Acropolis originally; however, by the time it was fortified it had spread all round, forming, in the words of Herodotos, a 'wheel-shaped city' (7.140.2) with the Acropolis as hub.

Like many older Greek communities, Athens had grown around an acropolis several kilometres inland 'in order to protect themselves from piracy' (Thucydides 1.7.1). Later, when the need for an outlet to the sea was imperative, the nearest suitable point on the Attic coast was developed. Flourishing to become a sort of duplicate city, the Peiraieus lay some 6km to the south-west, a low rocky peninsula (Akte) with three well-protected, deep, natural harbours (Kantharos, Zea and Mounychia). Here ship sheds housed the triremes of Athens' fleet.

Chronology

Thucydides reports the hasty erection of the city walls 'in all directions' (1.93.2), which indicates an attempt to enclose the whole urban area of Athens. In 478 BC, following the defeat of Xerxes, the Spartans had not only urged the Athenians to refrain from building their own fortifications, but also wanted all Greek *poleis* outside of the Peloponnese to demolish their existing fortifications. Themistokles held the Spartans off with foot-dragging diplomacy, having instructed the Athenians to raise a circuit. And so, according to Thucydides (1.90.3), no public building and no private house were to be spared, and everything that could be of use in the fortifications was torn down. The rushed work and the use of old material, including grave markers, is evident in the remains themselves, but the truth behind the story must be that

Athens and the Peiraieus (431 BC)

In its war with Sparta, Athens came to depend on grain from the Greek communities on the Black Sea littoral, but the Long Walls connecting the city to the Peiraieus enabled the Athenians to keep contact with their naval and merchant vessels even when besieged. Only the defeat of the war-fleet and the threat of starvation would force them to capitulate. However, thanks to Persian gold, Sparta finally gained the upper hand when Admiral Lysandros resoundingly defeated the Athenians at Aigospotami (summer 405 BC). The following spring Lysandros was able to strangle Athens into submission, his victory in the Hellespont having effectively cut the Athenian sea route from the Black Sea. In spite of its formidable navy, and the erection of the Long Walls, the reliance upon seaborne supply turned out to be Athens' Achilles heel.

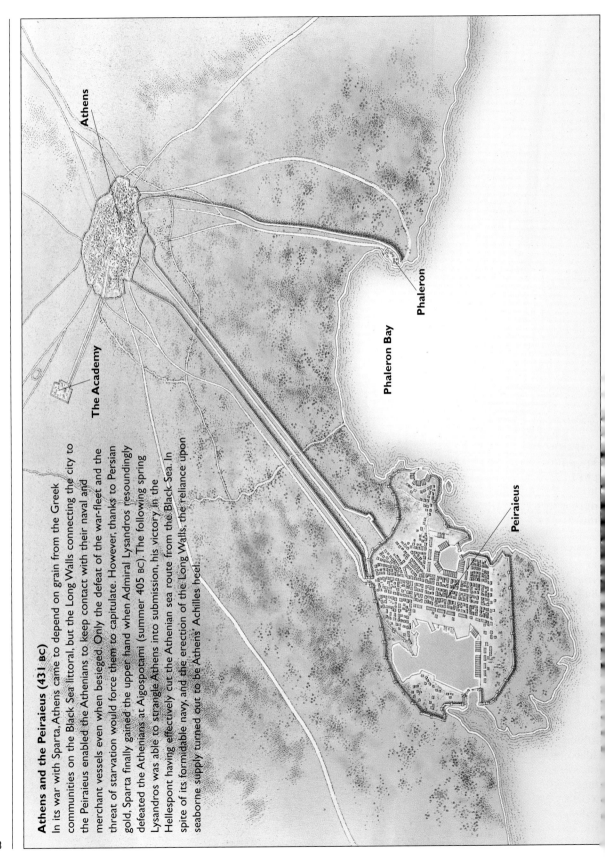

Athens

The Academy

Phaleron

Phaleron Bay

Peiraieus

some of the walls were thrown together so that the city could be defended at a pinch, and that when the threat passed they were completed at greater leisure. It is, of course, all part of the Themistokles myth. No doubt Thucydides was right to characterize the great man as 'supreme at doing precisely the right thing at precisely the right moment' (1.138.3).

With the city itself secure, Themistokles then persuaded the Athenians to complete the development and fortifications of the Peiraieus, which, according to Thucydides (1.93.3), had started during Themistokles' archonship of 493 BC. Thucydides adds (1.93.5) that this circuit was unusual even in the author's day. Built entirely of squared blocks, doweled and clamped together, the walls were so high and thick that they could be defended by a relatively small number of second-rate troops.

The Themistoklean circuit (phase 1) was to protect Athens throughout the Peloponnesian War, which pitted Athens and its empire against Sparta and its allies (known collectively as the Peloponnesians). The Long Walls, sometimes called 'legs' (*skéle*, Plutarch *Kimon* 13.7), were added before this conflict, first laid out under Kimon and completed under Perikles (*c.*458–440 BC). Initially there were two long walls (Thucydides 1.107.1), one (north) running from Athens to the Peiraieus, the other (Phaleric) to Phaleron, a broad open bay and site of Athens' earliest harbour (Herodotos 6.116). Later a third (south) long wall was added, the 'middle wall', about 180m from and parallel to the first City–Peiraieus wall (Plato *Gorgias* 455e with scholion = Fornara 79A). Between these walls was a roadway. Another, probably the carriage-road mentioned by Xenophon (*Hellenika* 2.4.10), ran outside the northern wall. These fortifications, built of well-cut ashlar masonry, were an important element in Athenian naval strategy, securely joining landlocked Athens to the three fortified harbours of its port. The total circuit of Athens (City Wall), the Long Walls, and the Peiraieus

ABOVE LEFT The City Wall survives as successive socles, seen here in two courses of poros blocks (Themistoklean socle) and one of well-jointed polygonal blocks in blue limestone (Kononian socle). Above, in creamy limestone, are two courses from the rebuilding of 307–304 BC. (Author's collection)

ABOVE RIGHT The Sacred Gate spanned the Sacred Way and the Eridanos, the stream carried by a vaulted channel (right). The forecourt, with inner and outer passages, is 18m deep, with a wall on the flank opposite the channel and corner towers. (Author's collection)

was over 30km (178 *stadia*, Thucydides 2.13.7), which made the Athenians virtually impregnable to siege provided they retained control of the sea.

Having recovered from the defeat by Sparta, Konon, with Persian gold, was able to rebuild sections of the Long Walls and the City Wall (phase 2) torn down at the end of the Peloponnesian War (Xenophon *Hellenika* 2.2.20, 23, 4.8.9–10). Several inscriptions have been found recording payments to contractors for material and labour for different sections of these fortifications. They are dated by year, from 393 BC to 390 BC, and were apparently actually set into the brickwork. However, the rebuilding work was probably finished only after 346 BC (Demosthenes 19.125, cf. Xenophon *Poroi* 6.1).

Possible repairs to the fortifications took place in order to protect Athens against the Macedonians after Chaironeia (338 BC). The great haste with which this building work was executed is reminiscent of the original Themistoklean circuit, and contemporary speeches imply it was completed in a similar fashion (Lykourgos *Against Leokrates* 44, Aischines 3.236). It is perhaps at this time that the outer wall (*proteichisma*) and ditch were added outside the original line. The expected attack, however, did not take place.

Demetrios Poliorketes, having 'liberated' Athens from Kassandros' garrison (Plutarch *Demetrios* 8–10), completely overhauled the City Wall (phase 3), while at the same time the Dipylon Gate and *proteichisma* were rebuilt from the ground up (307–304 BC). The building decree of 307/306 BC not only covers repairs to the existing brickwork but also gives specifications for rebuilding the City Wall, including the roofing of the wall-walk or *parodos* (*IG* ii^2 463.52–74 = Harding 134). Winter (1971: 141) sees the roofed *parodos* as the simplest means of protecting from the elements the small torsion-spring catapults, probably bolt-shooters, mounted on the curtains: the Athenians were certainly building torsion artillery by 306/305 BC (*IG* ii^2 1487B.84–90, cf. 1467B.48–56, 1627B.328–329). The improved fortifications enabled the Athenians to withstand the siege mounted by Kassandros in 304 BC (Plutarch *Demetrios* 23.1).

Calibration of bolts for bolt-shooter (*katapéltes oxybelés*)	
1-cubit	1 cubit (*pechys*) – 462.4mm (18.21in.)
1.5-cubit	Most popular machine, firing a bolt *c*.400m
2-cubit	
3-cubit	
4-cubit	Maximum length for bolts
Note: maximum effective range was achieved through setting machine's elevation at 30 degrees	

Limestone column drums from the Peisistratid temple of Olympian Zeus. The project was abandoned when the tyrants were expelled in 510 BC, and these un-fluted drums ended up in the Themistoklean socle of the City Wall, hastily erected in 478 BC. (Author's collection)

Circuit

The construction method remained basically the same until the mid-6th century AD. A low socle, some 2.5m wide and rising 1m above ground level, was built of an inner and outer skin of dressed masonry laid in fairly regular courses, the space between then filled with earth and rubble. This structure supported a 7 or 8m-high wall of sun-dried mud-bricks. Upon completion, the whole surface of the brick superstructure was smoothed with mud and plastered with clay or lime to prevent rainwater from percolating into the joints. This vital process of plastering the brickwork is well attested in 4th-century Athenian documents (*IG* ii^2 167.82–84, 463.81–85, 106–109, 1663, 1664), and Demosthenes berates a political rival for squandering state funds on 'the battlements, which we are coating with lime plasters' (3.29 with scholion).

Such battlements were probably in the form of a crenellated parapet that protected a *parodos*. To prevent rainwater from collecting along the top of the brickwork, and thus dangerously weakening it, the parapet would be covered in terracotta coping tiles set on a layer of clay and straw (e.g. Thucydides 3.22.4). The *parodos*, however, required a more durable paving of slabs. The Athenian inscription of 307/306 BC ordains that the *parodos* and other portions subjected to wear be given a hard covering (possibly stone) imposed on a 'finger-thickness of sieved earth' (*IG* ii^2 463.81–85). The circuit itself was reinforced at vital points with two-storeyed towers some 5m square. About 15 gateways, of which 10 are known for certain, and a number of posterns also pierced it.

The circuit was rebuilt several times over the centuries. In reconditioning a wall, the brickwork was usually removed or levelled down and the old socle was brought higher – due to the rising street levels – by superimposing a new socle. New brickwork was then laid on top. The building-document of 307/306 BC orders the restoration work to include binding the decaying brickwork with 'wooden baulks' (*IG* ii^2 463.74–75). This certainly figured in a makeshift addition to the fortifications of Plataia, thereby 'preventing the structure from becoming weak as it attained height' (Thucydides 2.75.5, cf. Philon *Paraskeuastika* 1.13 [oak], Vitruvius 1.53 [charred olive]).

City Wall			
Phase 1	478 BC	Themistoklean socle	Four courses (rubble > polygonal); possible that uppermost course (polygonal: quarry) belongs to the c.420 BC repairs
Phase 2	393–390 BC	Kononian socle	One course blue Peiraieic limestone (coursed polygonal: broached > pointed, bevelled); possible repairs 338 BC
Phase 3	307–304 BC	Hellenistic socle	Two courses poros stretchers, reused blocks and small stone fillers (quite regular isodomic ashlar: quarry)

Sacred Gate

It was here that the procession for the goddess Demeter gathered before it made its way along the Sacred Way from Athens to Eleusis. The name 'Sacred Gate' (*hiera pyle*) does not appear in the literary sources before Plutarch, who writes that Sulla's troops broke through the curtain 'between the Sacred Gate and the Peiraieic Gate' (*Sulla* 14.5, cf. Appian *Mithridateios* 149) and thus took Athens and laid it to waste (86 BC). However, Sacred Gate, like Sacred Way, is probably a much older name.

The Sacred Gate was a forecourt gateway with four rectangular flanking towers, the entranceway being recessed some 18m behind the line of the City Wall and furnished with two passages, one for the Eridanos stream, and one for the Sacred Way. Attackers would have been compelled to advance along the latter passage, shut in between the southern flanking wall and the stream, with their right (unshielded) side, moreover, exposed to flanking fire from the top of the wall along the northern bank.

The Dipylon Gate sits at the end of a forecourt, open on the west and protected by four corner towers and two flanking walls. A central pier separates the double gates. The outer, vaulted gates were added in the 1st century BC. (Author's collection)

Sacred Gate

Phase 1	478 BC	Themistoklean gateway	Two entrances with forecourt, each crowned with *parodos* to defend passage of Eridanos and street separately; socle of two foundation courses poros, and two upper courses hard limestone; repairs *c*.420 BC
Phase 2	393–390 BC	Kononian gateway	Extensive alterations: Eridanos re-channelled to provide a wider street; bastion built (concept of separate defence for stream and street abandoned); socle of three courses reddish limestone (headers & stretchers: quarry > tooled, drafted margins); possible repairs 338 BC
Phase 3	307–304 BC	Hellenistic gateway	Complete overhaul: larger corner towers, fenestrated and gable-roofed (i.e. artillery)

Dipylon Gate

The term 'Dipylon' first appears in a decree (*IG* ii² 673B.4) dated to 278/277 BC; originally the gateway was called the Thriasian Gate (or Gates) as the road out of it led to the Thriasian plain at Eleusis (Harpokration *Lexicon s.v.* Anthemokritos, cf. Isaios [Forster fr. 24]). This forecourt gateway, the largest in Greece (1,800m²), was the principal entrance of Athens. The fact that it was used during the Panathenaic Festival is probably the main reason for its size.

The Panathenaic procession assembled beside the gateway, and possibly in the forecourt itself. According to an inscribed document (*IG* ii² 334.24–25), the meat from the great sacrifice to Athena, the hecatomb, was distributed here. Large numbers of postholes have been found in the forecourt and it seems that these would have supported the tents in which the Athenians feasted. Likewise, as the arterial roads to Thebes and Corinth started here, the spacious forecourt served as a convenient meeting and departure point. Here travellers could purchase last minute provisions or souvenirs from hustlers, or refresh themselves and their animals at the nearby fountain house. The Roman satirist Lucian records (*Dialogues of the Courtesans* 4.3) that lovers often scribbled their erotic greetings on the forecourt walls.

Obviously contrived to impress citizens and visitors alike, the Dipylon Gate also had the potential to frustrate would-be attackers. The forecourt was covered at each of its four corners by rectangular towers, and between these ran two flank walls each crowned by a *parodos*. In wartime, therefore, this cul-de-sac functioned as a deadly trap for anyone approaching with hostile intent, subjecting attackers to crossfire in every direction from high up, as were, for example, the penned troops of Philip V of Macedon when they attempted to storm Athens in 200 BC (Livy 31.24.9–16).

Although the ground plan essentially remains the same throughout, the Dipylon Gate does exhibit two major building phases, the construction phase of 478 BC and a rebuilding at the end of the 4th century BC. Initially a single pair of gates located at the inner end of the cul-de-sac – hence the term 'Dipylon' – secured the Themistoklean gateway. In the late Hellenistic period, however, a second pair of vaulted gates was added to the front, thereby converting the cul-de-sac into a cage.

Dipylon Gate			
Phase 1	478 BC	Themistoklean gateway	Inner double gate (non-vaulted); four small rectangular corner towers with left-front (Tower C) projecting on unshielded side; poros socle, mud-brick superstructure
Phase 2	307–304 BC	Hellenistic gateway	Same plan but solid construction (i.e. artillery) in conglomerate blocks sheathed with blue Peiraieic limestone; larger corner towers, fenestrated and gable-roofed

This marble altar stands behind the Dipylon Gate. It is dedicated to Zeus Herkeios (protector of forecourts), Hermes (guardian of travellers) and the eponymous hero Akamas, honoured because the gateway lies in the Kerameikós, a *deme* belonging to the tribe Akamantis. (Author's collection)

The *proteichisma* (right) and ditch, now partially back-filled, associated with it. Added after Chaironeia, this stone outwork made it difficult for besiegers to bring siege equipment too close to the Themistoklean circuit. (Author's collection)

Proteichisma

This was an outer line of defence 7 to 8m forward of the Themistoklean circuit, consisting of a stone wall (conglomerate: alternating headers and stretchers) and the ditch, rectangular in section and about 8m wide and 4m deep, associated with it. With the development of mechanical warfare by the Macedonians the function of combined ditch and breastwork is best seen as a more positive countermeasure, other than by sallying forth and physically destroying them, of keeping mobile siege machines away from the City Wall, or at least slowing down their approach. Additionally, the ditch would have served as an effective deterrent to mining.

The *proteichisma*, however, would not have afforded the City Wall much protection against artillery as it still lay within the effective range of enemy machines mounted on the outer edge of the defensive system. As already noted, one of the aims of the building programme of 307/306 BC was to provide for the mounting of torsion-spring catapults on the curtains to keep the attacker's machines as far away from the City Wall as possible. The confines of the *parodos* limited the size of these catapults, but the height of their placement ensured that they could often target larger besieging machines, especially the stone-throwing variety, before their own walls were in range. Military engineers

Calibration of stone-shot for stone-thrower **(*katapéltes lithobólos*)**	
Δ	10 *minae*
ΔΕ	15 *minae*
ΔΔ	20 *minae*
ΔΔΔ	30 *minae*
ΔΔΔΔ	40 *minae*
T	1 talent (*tálanton*) = 60 *minae*
ΔT	10 *minae* plus 1 talent (i.e. 70 *minae*)

The above calibres are based on the 353 stones discovered outside the ancient circuit of Rhodes. These Rhodian shot of blue crystalline limestone were carefully inscribed with letters indicating their weight, most of which still show traces of red paint applied to the incisions to make the weight-marks readily visible. Calibration of shot was generally one of a graduated series, which rose by differences of 5 or 10 *minae* up to a common maximum of 60 *minae* by the mid-3rd century BC (Philon *Poliorkētika* 1.29, 70–73). Thirty-mina shot could be launched most effectively over ranges below 400m and, according to Philon (*fl*. 200 BC), 30-mina engines 'have the most appropriate dimensions and are most forceful in their blows' (*Poliorkētika* 96.10). For instance, on the basis of the shot found, the most popular calibres at Rhodes appear to have been those of 25 *minae* (85 shot) and 30 *minae* (83 shot).

Ring Street, viewed from Tower C, Dipylon Gate. This thoroughfare, which ran between the City Wall (right) and the *proteichisma* (left), encompassed Athens and gave access to its suburbs. Sokrates famously used it to get from the Academy to the Lykeion. (Author's collection)

working for Philip II of Macedon had succeeded in adding torsion to the catapult, thus making it possible to hurl large stones against city walls. Philip's first use of the torsion-spring catapult, at the sieges of Perinthos and Byzantium (340 BC), was unsuccessful (Diodoros 16.74.2–76.4, 77.2–3). Alexander would, however, later use it with greater success, as would the Successors of Alexander.

Any troops defending the breastwork would normally have been withdrawn through posterns in the main circuit if the *proteichisma* was in danger of being overrun. Between the circuit and the *proteichisma* the land sloped sharply, and here a dumped filling was thrown in to reinforce the *proteichisma* and provide an even level for a

thoroughfare for wheeled traffic, the so-called Ring Street. This road encircled the whole city and linked the suburbs. For Sokrates, according to Plato (*Lysias* 203a), this was the quickest route from the Academy to the Lykeion.

Stone shot (various calibres) for stone-throwers, Athenian Kerameikós. These stones are carefully shaped spheres, although rough stones were sometimes given a coating of clay to render them spherical, to ensure efficient ballistics. (Author's collection)

Gyphtokastro (Attica)

Abandoning the Periklean city-based defence strategy, the Athenians began building a series of pocket-sized frontier defences as a means to repel small raids and slow down the advance of a large invading force. The chief purpose of these strongholds, therefore, was to command a road, a particular strip of land, or a stretch of vulnerable coastline. Usually situated in remote regions that had no importance save from the military point of view, the circuit was generally very compact, and there was nothing inside the walls except barracks for housing troops and cisterns for storing rainwater. The border fort at Eleutherai, commonly Gyphtokastro ('gypsy castle'), in north-western Attica is typical of such military strongholds.

Topography

Gyphtokastro was built to crown a steep and rocky knoll on the south side of the Dryoskephalai (Káza) Pass, the major access route leading north–south between the Kithairon and Parnes ranges, and guarded the road from Thebes via Plataia to Athens. Anyone passing from central Greece to the Peloponnese had to come through this pass, which was known in antiquity as the 'road by

Dipylon Gate, Athens (304 BC)

Improvements in security led to the development of the forecourt gateway, of which the Dipylon Gate is a prime example. With its entrance set back from the line of the circuit, thus forming a three-sided enclosure or cul-de-sac, the forecourt gateway functioned as a deadly trap for attackers, who were subjected to enfilading fire from above. The 'Dipylon' was the double gate, as the name implies, located at the inner end of the cul-de-sac. Originally built in

478 BC as part of Themistokles' building programme, the gateway was completely rebuilt in stone under Demetrios Poliorketes. Although the original plan was retained, the gateway became a solid construction in conglomerate blocks sheathed with blue Peiraieic limestone. The towers also became much larger as well as fenestrated and gable-roofed, to allow for the provision of small torsion-spring catapults.

Gyphtokastro was strategically located above the Dryoskephalai Pass, the principal route leading north–south between Mount Parnes and Mount Kithairon, through which ran the highway from Athens to Plataia. The fort is seen here looking south-east from the modern road. (Author's collection)

Anyone wishing to pass from central Greece to the Peloponnese had to come through the Dryoskephalai (Káza) Pass. The pass is seen here looking north-west towards the Kithairon range from Tower 1 on the north wall of Gyphtokastro. (Author's collection)

Eleutherai' (Thucydides 3.24.2, Xenophon *Hellenika* 5.4.14, Arrian *Anabasis* 1.7.9, Pausanias 9.1.6, 2.1–2).

The town of Eleutherai itself, according to both Strabo (9.2.31) and Pausanias (1.38.8–9), at times belonged to Boiotia and at times to Athens. On the other hand, Diodoros (4.2.6, 3.1), Pliny (*Naturalis historia* 4.7.26) and Apollodoros (3.5.5) all refer to it as Boiotian. The status of Eleutherai at any one period is by no means clear. It seems likely that the Athenians had control late in the 6th century BC, probably after they defeated the Boiotians in 506 BC (*IG* i^3 501 = Fornara 42, Herodotos 5.77, cf. 6.108, Thucydides 3.55.1). In the following century a citizen from Eleutherai appears on an Athenian casualty list (*IG* i^2 943 11.96–97), but otherwise the little evidence we have suggests it was under Boiotian control. Both Herodotos (5.74.2) and Thucydides (2.18.2), for instance, recognize Oinoe – and not Eleutherai – as the limit of Attica.

Circuit

By the early 4th century BC, this strategic site had been furnished with a five-room blockhouse with thick walls built in a mannered polygonal masonry style with drafted margins. Somewhat later, probably soon after 370 BC, a proper circuit was erected. This followed the contours of the hillock closely and enclosed an area measuring roughly 100m north–south by 275m east–west. Well-built forecourt gateways opened toward the north–west and south–east, the former bearing a faint inscription indicating that it led to Plataia. Two posterns in the north wall and one in the south wall provided additional exits.

Athenian or Boiotian?

The fort features in discussions of the defences of Attica (Ober 1985: 160–163), though a case can be made that it is actually Boiotian, built when Epameinondas led the Thebans to the hegemony of Greece (371–362 BC). The trapezoidal masonry in hard grey limestone blocks with quarry faces finds its best parallels in Boiotia rather than Attica (Cooper 1986: 195, Harding 1988: 61–71, Camp 1991: 199–202, cf. Ober 1987: 601–603, 1989: 294–301). On the other hand, the north wall, studded with rectangular towers every 30m or so, faces towards Boiotia not Attica, and its defenders could fire projectiles at enemy soldiers coming through the pass. In comparison, the south wall has only three towers.

Across the plain some 5km to the south-east at Mazi stands the remains of a free-standing tower. This five-storey tower once commanded the route into

LEFT A good stretch of the north wall of Gyphtokastro stands well preserved, with rectangular towers every 30m or so. Seen here, looking east-south-east from the gravel track up to the site, are Towers 2 to 4. (Author's collection)

BELOW LEFT Towers 6 and 7 were first-generation artillery towers. Each consisted of two chambers above a solid base. The lower chamber was not for catapults – these were housed in the fenestrated upper chamber – but for archers. Tower 6 is seen here from Tower 7. (Author's collection)

Attica from the Dryoskephalai Pass. Along the same road and about 2.5km further north-east, was the fortified Attic *deme* of Oinoe (Myoupolis), which had been walled by the start of the Peloponnesian War at the latest (Thucydides 2.18.2). To the north-east, some 400m higher on Mount Parnes (Párnitha) and overlooking a fertile upland valley (Skourta plain), is the slight remains of the Attic border fort of Panakton (Kavasala). This stronghold was taken by treachery by the Boiotians during the Peloponnesian War and demolished before it was returned to the Athenians as part of the settlement of the Peace of Nikias in 422/421 BC (Thucydides 5.3.5, 18.7, 35.5, 36.2, 40.1–2, 42.1–2, 44.3, Plutarch *Alkibiades* 14.4). Several inscriptions (*IG* ii^2 1299, 1303–05, 2971, cf. Demosthenes 19.326, 54.3–5) mention the Athenian garrisons that manned the rebuilt fort during the 4th and 3rd centuries BC.

ABOVE Towers 2 to 5 have ground-floor chambers without loops or windows, and second chambers at *parodos* level with arrow slits. They were not, therefore, designed to house catapults but as battle-stations for archers. Tower 5 is seen here from Tower 4. (Author's collection)

Garrison

By the 370s BC (Aischines 2.167) the Athenians had introduced *ephebeia*, a two-year paramilitary service for all 18- and 19-year-old citizen youths or ephebes (*epheboi*). Following the defeat at Chaironeia (338 BC), *ephebeia* was formalized by Epikrates' law of 336/335 BC (Harpokration *Lexicon s.v.* Epikrates), and from then at least, if not before, service as an ephebe was not only compulsory but also involved garrison duty.

The Aristotelian *Athenaion politeia* (42.3–5) describes in detail the training ephebes underwent. The first year was taken up with a cycle of athletic contests, mainly footraces such as the *hoplitodromos*, a 400m race in which the competitors carried a hoplite shield and wore a helmet and, originally, greaves. There were also competitions for the *pyrrhiche* (pyrrhic dance), a kind of military ballet described by Plato as 'movements that evade blows and missiles by dodging, yielding, leaping, [and] crouching, and the opposite offensive postures of striking with missiles, arrows, and spears, and all sorts of blows' (*Laws* 815a). As well as using athletics as a military preparation, the ephebes also received from their instructors training in the use of hoplite weapons as well as the bow, the javelin and the sling (*Athenaion politeia* 42.3).

At the beginning of the second year the ephebes were issued, at state expense, a shield, a spear, a military cloak (*chlamys*) and a broad-brimmed hat (*petasos*). The ephebes were now ready to practise their newly acquired skills in the field. According to the *Athenaion politeia* (42.4) they provided permanent garrisons for the border forts and watchtowers. Some also patrolled the mountainous borderlands and were called *peripoloi* ('those who travel about'), as did the orator Aischines, who, after boyhood, 'became a *peripolos* of this *chōra* for two years' (2.167).

ABOVE LEFT The *parodos* running between Towers 3 and 4 on the north wall of Gyphtokastro. Seen here is the side door that gave access to the second chamber of Tower 4 from the *parodos*, which would have been protected by a crenellated parapet. (Author's collection)

ABOVE RIGHT The postern, external view, hard by Tower 2, north wall of Gyphtokastro. When used for sorties, troops leaving the fort would have had their right (unshielded) side covered by the tower and those stationed within. (Author's collection)

Attic border fort at Eleutherai

Athens had a series of outlying forts in various directions to protect its approaches by land. Gyphtokastro is a fine example of one of these. It was built to crown a steep-sided hillock guarding the road from Athens to Thebes. The circuit, of trapezoidal masonry in hard grey limestone, is fortified with a series of two-storeyed towers projecting inwards and outwards from the walls. Apart from Towers 6 and 7, which housed non-torsion catapults, a door at ground-floor level allowed access to each tower. A pair of doors at first-floor level led out on to the *parodoi*. The towers themselves had flat, wooden roofs, each protected by a parapet and thus serving as an open fighting platform.

Mantineia (Arcadia)

Following Sparta's defeat at Leuktra (371 BC) the scattered Mantineians, with Theban aid, returned to the city previously destroyed by the Spartan king Agesipolis. As well as raising the extensive fortifications whose ruins we see today, they also rearranged the course of the Ophis so that it became a defence instead of a danger. The Mantineians were obviously concerned with avoiding

a repetition of the disaster of 385 BC, when Agesipolis damned the river and the rising waters caused a stretch of the mud-brick fortifications to collapse.

Topography

The existence of Mantineia was important because the security of its city walls encouraged Mantineian autonomy in foreign policy and the development of an independent democratic political system that was hostile to Sparta (Xenophon *Hellenika* 5.2.1–2, cf. Thucydides 5.29.1). It was shortly after the Persian Wars, according to Strabo (8.3.2), that the Mantineians left their five village settlements (*kōmai*) and united as one *polis*, an event that can be linked with the establishment of democracy in Mantineia (Aristotle *Politics* 1318b4–5). If political and physical union (*synoikismos*) led to the adoption of a democratic constitution, then life in village settlements fostered oligarchic rule that encouraged loyalty to Sparta's own interests (Pausanias 8.8.9, 10, Xenophon *Hellenika* 5.2.7, 6.4.18, cf. 5.3–5).

As an artificial foundation Mantineia lacked an acropolis. Thus, albeit with some natural protection from a small river, the Mantineians built their city on what was, for Arcadia, practically level ground. Situated in eastern Arcadia, the *chōra* of the Mantiñeians was a bare upland plain (629m) enclosed by an amphitheatre of barren mountains. This alpine plain, whose terrain and location made it a convenient meeting place for armies, often became the cockpit in which pro- and anti-Spartan alliances settled their differences (418 BC, 370/369 BC, 362 BC).

ABOVE Aerial view of Mantineia looking south-west. The Tegea Gate (top left) is a fine example of gateway and tower arrangement. Note also the posterns in the flanks of the towers along the east wall. (Author's collection)

RIGHT An arrow slit in the front wall of the ground-floor chamber of Tower 2, Gyphtokastro. This was cut at a much later date (note repairs to stonework), as the tower originally lacked loops at this level. (Author's collection)

Circuit

The circuit of the re-founded city is elliptical in form, with a perimeter of nearly 4km enclosing an area of some 1.24km², and generally follows the same lines as its 5th-century predecessor (Scranton 1941: 57–59). The walls, encircled by the diverted Ophis except for a short distance on the south-east, were built out of mud-brick. The brickwork, some 4.05 to 5m in width, rested upon a high stone socle of large rectangular or polygonal blocks holding a fill of fieldstones and earth. Over 120 square towers reinforced the circuit, of which 118 have been traced, placed about 26m apart, and 10 gateways, mostly of the 'overlap' type, pierced its line. Gateways of this type did not have direct access, but were designed so that the entry ran more or less parallel to the circuit for several metres.

As Mantineia stood entirely on a level plain, it might be reasonable to expect the gateways to have been planned with flanking towers on the attacker's right (unshielded) side. Actually, the reverse is the case. It is true that at least some of the gateways had a second tower on the inner wall, just outside the entrance to the corridor. The placing of the primary tower on the attacker's left side, however, does suggest that even on level ground the major virtue of such gateways lay in compelling the enemy to advance for some distance below the line of the main wall.

An unusual feature for the 4th century BC – it would become fairly common in Hellenistic times – was the positioning of posterns in the flanks of towers. Promoted by Epameinondas, the Theban *stratēgos* and leading soldier of the day, new Mantineia probably incorporated in its defensive system all the most up-to-date ideas. The use of the Ophis as a wet moat encircling the city was a stroke of genius. Likewise, instead of placing posterns in the curtains under the shelter of a neighbouring tower, the designers cleverly incorporated them in

Mantineia's socle, of regular-coursed polygonal masonry, was exceptionally high owing to the wet nature of the terrain. The river Ophis ('snake') was re-routed so as to form a wet moat around the re-founded city. (Author's collection)

the ground-floor chambers of the towers themselves. Defending troops issuing from these openings would have been in greatest danger at the moment they emerged, while they were still in single file. To offset this as far as possible, the posterns were set in the right flank of the tower (facing the field). Thus the defenders, as they emerged, presented their shielded sides to the enemy.

Messene (Messenia)

After three centuries of enslavement by the Spartans, the Messenians were liberated by Epameinondas and reacquired their own *polis*; the foundation of Messene would be an outward and very visible sign of Sparta's humiliation. This was not the only post-Leuktra blow that Epameinondas was able to inflict on Sparta. He also supervised the construction of Megalopolis in southern Arcadia and initiated the re-founding of Mantineia. Messene, with Megalopolis and Mantineia, completed the strategic barrier to contain the Spartans.

Topography

Situated in the famously fertile Stenyklaros plain of Messenia (Tyrtaios [West fr. 5], Strabo 8.5.6), Messene sits in a hollow between three hills, Eva to the south-east, Psoriari to the west and Ithome to the north. The site is dominated by the summit of Ithome (802m), a natural stronghold and thus an obvious choice for an acropolis. Ithome ('step') had figured as a refuge in the First (c.736–716 BC) and Third (c.464–460 BC) Messenian wars.

Chronology

The literary evidence (Diodoros 15.66.1, 6, 67.1, Pausanias 4.27.5–7) imparts that the city was founded, and the building of the fortifications begun, in 369 BC under the auspices of Epameinondas. Having restored the Messenians to their territory, he actively encouraged

ABOVE Boiotians had a reputation as gluttonous boors, but Epameinondas was, in the opinion of a good judge (Sir Walter Raleigh), the greatest of the ancient Greeks. His four invasions of the Peloponnese resulted in the new cities of Messene, Megalopolis and Mantineia. (Author's collection)

RIGHT The west wall of Messene, looking east. The towers here are semicircular, as the 'Castle' (left), or rectangular, as Tower N (right). Semicircular towers are normally to be found at salient angles along the circuit. (Author's collection)

Messene

The circuit of Messene went up in the winter of 369 BC after Epameinondas invaded Sparta and then proceeded over Mount Taÿgetos to liberate Messenia. Built with incredible rapidity by the combined Theban and Argive armies, as well as the exiled Messenians who had been invited to return and establish an independent state, Messene was the southernmost link in a defensive chain of walled cities intended to keep the Spartans at bay. The

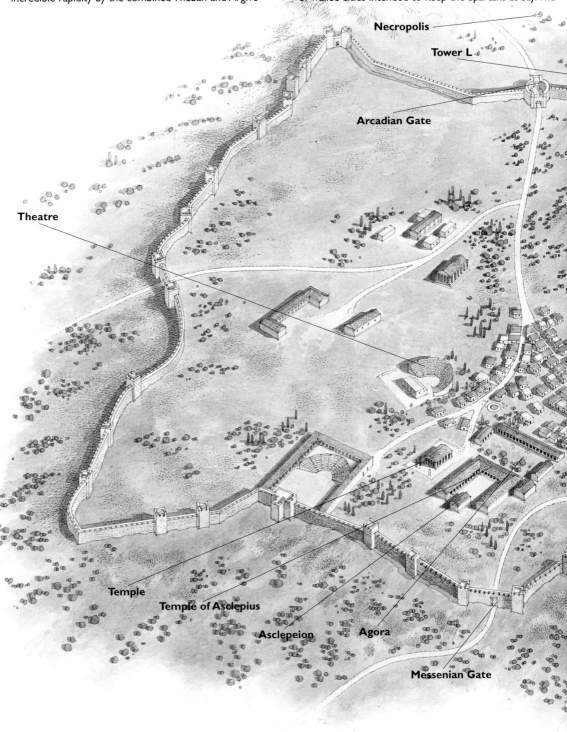

Necropolis

Tower L

Arcadian Gate

Theatre

Temple

Temple of Asclepius

Asclepeion

Agora

Messenian Gate

fortifications, the epitome of Greek military architecture, made use of the slopes of Mount Ithome and were designed to encompass enough open land for the citizens to rear livestock and cultivate crops. The walls, all stone built to a height of some 7 to 9m, were reinforced by projecting towers set at irregular intervals; resting on solid bases these were either one storey with windows or two storeys with loops in the lower and windows in the upper.

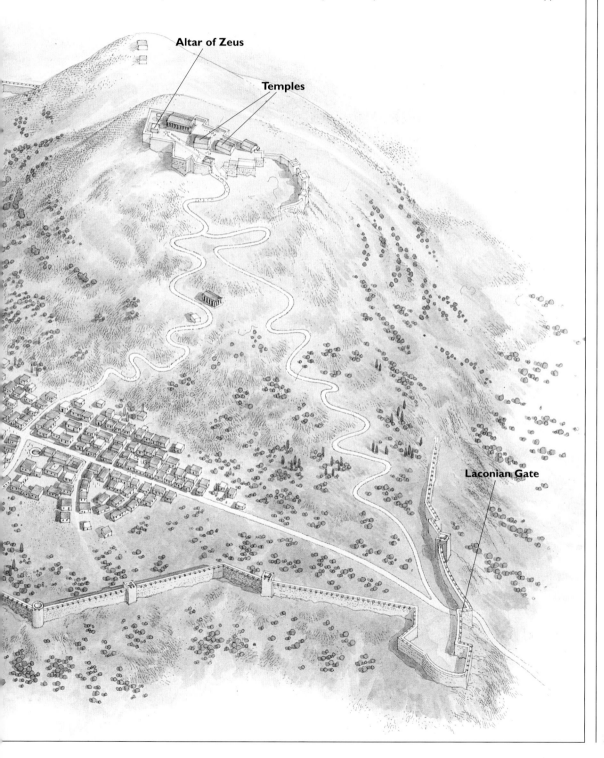

Altar of Zeus

Temples

Laconian Gate

The west wall of Messene, looking south towards Tower N. This structure is an excellent example of a first-generation artillery tower. Built with a solid base, the tower consisted of a single chamber, housing non-torsion catapults, surmounted by a fighting-platform roof. (Author's collection)

them to build city walls, a project apparently completed in a mere 85 days. Lawrence (1979: 382–85) argues coherently for a single main period of building, and his stand for an Epameinondean date for the circuit is supported by Ober (1987: 572). There are those, however, who advocate a considerably later date for the walls now visible. Marsden (1969: 127–38) has suggested, on stylistic grounds, that the north wall was a Hellenistic rebuilding.

Circuit

The rambling circuit, some 9.5km long, follows the line of the ridge descending from Ithome and was continuous except at various inaccessible points. Planned to enclose arable land, it doubtless served also as a refuge for the surrounding population in times of danger. Its stone walls consist of an outer and inner facing of un-mortared squared blocks, set some 2.5m apart and packed with a rubble core. The circuit is reinforced at irregular intervals (30–90m) by projecting towers. These are rectangular or, at salient angles, semicircular and are excellent examples of first-generation artillery towers.

Tower N, a well-preserved tower on the west wall, originally stood 9m high and consisted of a single chamber surmounted by a fighting platform, on a solid base. The masonry of the tower and associated curtain-wall is isodomic trapezoidal. Entry to the chamber was through two side doors from the *parodoi*, which ran behind crenellated parapets. The chamber has four small pentagonal windows that allowed for the provision of non-torsion catapults inside the tower. The windows, two in front and one in each sidewall, splay on the inside and thus resemble overlarge arrow slits.

Tower L, the best-preserved tower on the north wall, originally stood 12.5m high and consisted of two chambers above a solid base. The masonry of the tower and associated curtain-wall is isodomic ashlar. Entry into the tower was by a door in either sidewall of the lower chamber. The doors led to *parodoi* protected by crenellated parapets. Access to the upper chamber was probably via a ladder and trapdoor from the lower chamber. The lower chamber has four arrow slits, two in front and one in each sidewall, which splay internally. The upper chamber is equipped with four small rectangular windows, two in front and two in each

sidewall, which allowed for the provision of non-torsion catapults inside the tower. As open windows, unlike loops, had the disadvantage of exposing defenders to enemy missiles these were protected by double-leafed, outward-opening, side-swinging shutters attached to the outside of the tower wall.

The architects also dispensed with the fighting-platform roof and instead employed a gabled roof, which was easier to make watertight and thus keep machines dry. The fighting platforms at towers along the west wall allowed the defenders to fire upon enemy troops who approached close enough to the circuit to be outside the beaten zone of catapults, which could not be depressed much below the horizontal. Presumably in the case of the gable-roofed towers of the north wall, the designers felt that bolts fired laterally from neighbouring towers, in conjunction with hand-fired missiles shot by defenders on the *parodoi*, would provide adequate security against this particular threat.

Arcadian Gate
Of the four gateways that have been distinguished, the Arcadian Gate is the most impressive. Gateways in general provided both problems (since they

ABOVE LEFT One of the two side doors of the 'Castle', Messene. The enormous circuit made use of the slopes of three hills – here it climbs Psoriari – and was designed to envelop enough open land to enable the inhabitants to raise crops and livestock. (Author's collection)

ABOVE RIGHT Tower L, north wall of Messene. When chambers for artillery surmounted towers, roofs were necessary to keep the machines within dry. A gabled roof, as here, was easier to make watertight than a fighting-platform roof. (Author's collection)

constitute an obvious weakness in any fortification system) and opportunities for monumental embellishment as here with the Arcadian Gate.

The gateway consists of an outer and inner entrance, separated by a circular forecourt. Square towers, 10m apart, flanked the outer entrance, which is almost 5m wide. The forecourt, 19m in diameter, is still remarkable for the perfection of its masonry, laid dry on a base of two massive courses. On either side, near the outer entrance, is a niche for the protecting deities, one doubtless the Hermes noted by Pausanias (4.33.3). The inner entrance was in the form of a pair of two-leaved gates separated by a central post, an enormous monolith now partly fallen. All the evidence suggests that the gateway was totally demolished and rebuilt on a larger and more complex scale sometime around 300 BC (Scranton 1941: 128–29).

Other fortifications

Aigosthena (Megarid)

Aigosthena is at the eastern end of the Corinthian Gulf on the slopes of Mount Kithairon. The settlement, which certainly existed by the 8th century BC, was in the territory of Megara and, although rather remote, controlled the direct but difficult route between Boiotia and the Peloponnese. Xenophon (*Hellenika* 5.4.18, 6.4.26) records that the Spartans passed through Aigosthena in 378 BC and after their defeat at Leuktra in 371 BC. Aigosthena is seldom mentioned otherwise and consequently it is not clear when and why the fortifications were built. Dates in the mid-4th century BC (Megarian with Athenian aid), the late 4th century BC (Demetrios Poliorketes), and the mid-3rd century BC (Achaian League) have been proposed on the basis of their architectural style.

Tower L, Messene

The walls of Messene are considered the finest example of 4th-century military architecture, and by the second-quarter of the century Greek engineers had designed towers to accommodate artillery that shot from shuttered windows. The confines of the towers and small apertures of the windows limited the size of the catapults, but the great attitude of their placement more than made up for this and ensured that they could often target larger besieging engines before their own walls were in range. The upper windows were larger to allow small non-torsion catapults to fire from them, but the lower ones were just loops for archers. The roof was gabled to keep the machines dry, while the base was solid so as to support their weight. The masonry of the tower was isodomic ashlar in hard grey limestone.

ABOVE LEFT The Arcadian Gate, north wall of Messene, looking east towards Tower L. This had double entranceways separated by an enclosed circular forecourt in which an enemy who had penetrated would be trapped. Flanking towers strengthened the system further. (Author's collection)

ABOVE RIGHT Tower A, Aigosthena. Once three storeys high, the top chamber housed torsion catapults behind six shuttered windows. Archers were stationed on the two storeys below. The tower had a gabled roof and a solid base. (Author's collection)

The best-preserved section of the fortifications, which enclosed a rectangle some 550 by 180m, is on the east side of the acropolis. Tower A, at the south-eastern angle of the circuit and built of limestone and reddish conglomerate, was 9m² and 18m high. Just beneath the gabled roof were six shuttered windows, clearly discernible until the earthquake of 1981, evidently for catapults. Archers were stationed on the two storeys below and the tower had a solid base. Ashlar isodomic masonry was used for the towers (eight in total), mostly trapezoidal with occasional polygonal blocks for the curtains. The main gateway was by Tower F, between the acropolis and fortified lower city, while a postern stood between towers B and C on the outer east wall. Few traces of the wall on the south side of the lower city are evident, but the north wall is still *in situ* and runs down to the sea, a distance of some 450m, and is studded with eight rectangular towers and pierced by two gateways.

Eleusis (Attica)

Ancient Eleusis lies on the shore of a large bay 21km west of Athens. It was an important *deme* site at the edge of the Thriasian plain as well as the location of a sanctuary dedicated to Demeter, the goddess of corn. Her cult, the Eleusinian Mysteries, was one of the most successful in the Greek world and for a time rivalled Christianity in popularity.

Eleusis was the westernmost Attic *deme* and thus something of an outpost facing the Peloponnese, home of such long-standing enemies as the Megarians, Corinthians and Spartans. The sanctuary itself was protected by substantial

At Eleusis the tyrant Peisistratos (d. 527 BC) enclosed the sanctuary of Demeter with a substantial circuit. This was built with a low socle of limestone blocks set in polygonal style, which carried several metres of sun-dried mud-brick. (Author's collection)

fortifications, which had several building phases, starting in the mid-6th century BC under the Peisistratid tyrants of Athens. The acropolis was also walled, and Eleusis was one of the principal Attic border forts from at least as early as the 4th century BC.

The Peisistratid circuit replaced and extended an earlier Geometric circuit (c.750 BC) with much stronger walls of sun-dried mud-brick on a polygonal stone socle. A Persian breach in the brickwork was repaired under Kimon (479–461 BC) with limestone masonry in alternately wide and narrow courses (pseudo-isodomic), based directly on the Peisistratid socle. The circuit was extended under Perikles, and again in the 4th century BC. The so-called Lykourgan Wall (c.370–360 BC) was a socle of four slightly receding courses in pecked Eleusinian stone upon which were set tooled courses of yellow poros. This was probably a conscious matching of the earlier Periklean style. Both extensions also utilized circular corner-towers.

A Persian breach in the Peisistratid circuit was repaired, under Kimon, with limestone masonry. For the Persians' 'furthest west in Europe' (Herodotos 9.14) was marked by a raid into the Megarid, sacking Eleusis en route. (Author's collection)

At Eleusis the fortifications were extended under Perikles and again in the 4th century BC. This is the 'Lykourgan Wall' (370–360 BC), a socle of four courses in pecked Eleusinian stone upon which sit tooled courses of softer yellow poros. (Author's collection)

LEFT A common, cheap and effective building material, ancient mud-brick rarely survives today. Here we see 'melted' brickwork resting on a socle of 'Lesbian masonry', the North Tower of the West Gate, Eretria. (Author's collection)

BELOW The circular tower, north wall of the fort at Phyle. Such towers, according to Vitruvius (1.5.5), are more resistant to battering rams. They also, as here, provided the defence with better fields of fire. (Author's collection)

Eretria (Euboia)

Eretria, next to Chalkis, was the principal *polis* of Euboia. The second largest island in the Aegean, Euboia extends north-west to south-east for over 150km almost parallel (and close) to the mainland of central Greece and was, from the late 5th century BC onwards, joined to Boiotia by a succession of bridges across the narrow Euripos channel.

Eretria was founded (*c*.825 BC) on a strategic site with acropolis, natural harbour, access to fertile land, and control of the island's main east–west land route. Close political ties with Athens began in the 6th century BC. In retribution for aiding the revolt of Persia's Greek subjects (498 BC), a Persian expedition captured and sacked the city (490 BC). Eretria now entered the Athens-dominated ambit of the Delian League, later revolting (447/446 BC), whereupon the Athenians occupied it until it revolted again (411 BC).

The West Gate was strategically sited at the point where the artery from Chalkis crossed a winter torrent, originally by means of a ford. A gateway already existed in late archaic times, along with the first (wooden) bridge. The extant remains, however, are those of a rebuild after the Persian sack to a new design, renovated at the end of Athenian occupation (411 BC), in which the torrent bed now acted in effect as a moat. A stone bridge led the road through a bottleneck forecourt, flanked by a pair of bastion-like towers with mud-brick cores, to a two-leaved wooden gate. A well-preserved stretch of the circuit, punctuated by three rectangular towers, runs southward from the West Gate. The polygonal socle, dated to *c*.400 BC, once supported a mud-brick superstructure. The circuit as a whole enclosed an area from the shore to the summit of the acropolis to the north.

The east wall of Sounion, looking north towards the bay of Sounion from Tower 4. The high headland, dedicated to Poseidon, was fortified in 413/412 BC, and thereafter became an important garrison for the Athenians. (Author's collection)

Phyle (Attica)

We first hear of Phyle in the winter of 404/403 BC when Athens was under the heel of the Thirty Tyrants. One of their opponents, Thrasyboulos, occupied Phyle, a naturally defensible site according to Xenophon (*chorion*, *Hellenika* 2.4.2), with his band of 70 democrats. As Phyle was a strategic site on Mount Parnes, a border fort was planted there sometime in the early 4th century BC. This was garrisoned by ephebes during their second year of paramilitary service.

The fort was constructed on a triangular rocky crag (649m) that falls sheer on all sides, especially precipitous on the west and north. The site overlooks the most direct north–south route from Athens, some 20km to the south, to Boiotia. From it the view commands nearly the whole of the Attic plain.

The plan is a loose pentagon, though the fortifications themselves only encircle the eastern half of the crag. Surviving to their paved *parodoi*, the ashlar-masonry walls are broken at intervals by four towers, one of them circular, and two gateways. Within the defences were the barracks in which the ephebes ate and slept.

Sounion (Attica)

The 'sacred cape of Sounion' is first mentioned in Homer (*Odyssey* 3.278–83) as the place where Phrontis, Menelaos' helmsman, is buried. Lying at the southernmost tip of Attica, the cape is a precipitous rocky headland overlooking the Saronic Gulf. On its highest point (60m) stands the temple of Poseidon (*c.*440–430 BC) – this was the last landfall before sailors faced the Aegean – remembered as one of the most romantic ruins in Greece, painted by Turner and celebrated by Byron (*Don Juan* canto III stanza L16).

With the Spartans at Dekeleia, the overland route through Oropos to Euboia was cut. Since the beginning of the Peloponnesian War most of the Athenian livestock had been pastured on Euboia, from which they received essential supplies. Thus, in the winter of 413/412 BC, the Athenians fortified Sounion to protect the sea route to Euboia and the Black Sea, source of so much imported grain (Thucydides 8.4, cf. Xenophon *Hellenika* 5.1.23).

Forming a semicircle from the bay of Sounion on the north-west to the cliff edge on the south, the walls, complete with rectangular towers, enclosed the whole acropolis. Later, when Athens and other Greek states attempted to shake off Macedonian domination (Chremonidean War, 268/267–263/262 BC), the Athenians expanded and strengthened the fortifications. The new sections of the walls and a huge artillery bastion built to carry catapults show the characteristic signs of hasty construction: many of the marble blocks came from plundered grave monuments.

The artillery bastion, which was later inserted into the east wall of Sounion. Built of local Agrileza marble, many of the structure blocks come from plundered grave monuments. (Author's collection)

Nature of conflict and society

Plato judges that one facet of virtue is to be found in the traditional contest of hoplites facing each other in open battle. The use of walls as a protection is therefore 'unnatural' and can only lead to the deterioration of the moral character of the citizen of his state (*Laws* 778d4–79a7). Plato was particularly averse to city-based defence. He reviles Themistokles, Kimon and Perikles for having 'glutted Athens with harbours and dockyards and walls and tribute and rubbish of that sort' (*Gorgias* 519a). This conservative view that city walls do not make a state is to be found in other 4th-century writers as well, for instance Xenophon (*Oikonomikos* 5.4–5, 6.6–7, 10) and Isokrates (7.13, cf. 8.77, 84). Even Thucydides, despite his enthusiastic support for Perikles' city-based system of defence (1.143.5, cf. [Xenophon] *Athenaion politeia* 2.14–16), has Nikias say, 'men make the *polis* and not walls' (7.77, cf. Alkaios [Page frs. 28, 29]).

Apart from Athens, which could field some 13,000 citizen-hoplites – besides 16,000 above and below military age who garrisoned the border forts and manned the city walls – at the outbreak of the Peloponnesian War (Thucydides 2.13.6–7, 31.2), the greater majority of *poleis* had citizen populations of less than 5,000. In a far-reaching study Ruschenbusch (1984: 55–57) has counted some 750 *poleis* in the core area of the Greek world alone. Additionally, he (1985: 253–63) calculates that a 'typical *polis*' had a territory of only 25 to 100km^2 (Athens was *c*.2,400km^2) and an adult male citizen membership of no more than 133 to 800.

Take for instance Corinth, which appears to be typical of a *polis* where political power remained traditionally in the hands of the elite few (*oligoi*, hence 'oligarchy') and, as such, shows a remarkably stable history. At Plataia (479 BC), which was considered by the Greeks an all-out effort against the invading Persians, the *polis* fielded around 5,000 hoplites (Herodotos 9.28.3). For the battle fought in the vicinity of the river Nemea (394 BC), a location within Corinthian territory, the *polis* only mustered 3,000 hoplites (Xenophon *Hellenika* 4.2.17). In comparison, for Plataia Aigina had sent some 500 hoplites (Herodotos 9.28.6), while at the Nemea, fighting for the Spartans against the Corinthians and their allies, the combined strength of the hoplite contingents from the Argolid *poleis* of Epidauros, Troezen, Hermione and Halieis was 3,000 (Xenophon *Hellenika* 4.2.16).

The *polis*, quintessentially a 'guild of warriors', deployed its citizen body in a phalanx. This mass formation was an effective way of expressing military power. The phalanx is seen here on the Nereid monument, an early 4th-century tomb from Xanthos, Lycia. (Author's collection)

Like that of his former mentor, Aristotle's ideal state was still essentially a hoplite oligarchy (*Politics* 1279b4, 1294a–b, 1295a–297b), but he knew Plato's authoritarian dream of an un-walled city was totally obsolete because of the recent improvements in the efficiency of artillery and siege machines (*Politics* 1331a9–10). Despite his common-sense view, however, he retained vestiges himself of the traditional hoplite ideology (*Politics* 1330b9):

Doubtless there is something dishonourable in seeking safety behind strong walls, at any rate against an enemy equal in number or only very slightly superior.

And so the defenders came out from their city walls not because they had to, but because they accepted a code of military behaviour that made the risk of death in a short battle in an open field seem preferable to the protracted and indecisive struggle between inefficient attacker and unwilling defender. Since they 'played by the rules' and seldom locked themselves in, Greeks had little need of the tactics or the technology suited to siegecraft.

Agrarian city-state

The armies of Greek *poleis* were based on a levy of those citizens prosperous enough to equip themselves as hoplites, heavily armoured warriors who fought shoulder to shoulder in a large formation known as a phalanx (*phalanges*, 'stacks'). Except for Sparta, whose warriors were acknowledged as the 'craftsmen of war' (Xenophon *Lakedaimonion politeia* 13.5) because they devoted their entire lives to military training, and a few state-sponsored units such as the Sacred Band (*hieros lochos*) of Thebes, these citizen levies were untrained soldier-farmers who saw it as their moral, social and political duty to fight on behalf of their *polis*.

Hoplites were the citizens in battle; citizens were the hoplites in assembly. They went into battle not for fear of punishment or in hope of plunder and booty. They fought with neighbours, brothers, fathers, sons, uncles and cousins. This meant that they did their utmost to demonstrate courage, side-by-side with their comrades, and that they had a vested interest in the outcome. This was the unseen glue that bound the phalanx, and the *polis*, together. Only those who clashed with ashen spear and bronze shield, defying death and disdaining retreat, were deemed worthy.

Hoplite warfare

At first sight it may seem surprising that when Greek warfare emerges into the light of history, it not only soon becomes dominated by close-packed, heavily armoured amateurs, but also continues to be so for some three centuries (*c*.675–350 BC). It lasted so long because as time passed the system was maintained for the sake of tradition, shared values and social prejudice. Since hoplites were expected to provide their own equipment, the majority of the population in any given *polis* was necessarily excluded. But the full rights of citizenship were only accorded to those who could afford to take their place in the phalanx, so that the hoplites effectively were the 'nation in arms', and it would have been unthinkable to arm the *hoi polloí*. It was only in Athens, where the navy became important, that the poorest citizens, the *thêtes* who rowed the triremes, came to have a significant military role – hence Athenian democracy (*demokratia*: 'the people' [*dêmos*] 'rule' [*kratei*]), or what Aristotle aptly called 'trireme democracy' (*Politics* 1291b21, cf. 1304a8, 1321a2, [Xenophon] *Athenaion politeia* 1.2). Finally, as the events of the two Persian invasions of Greece (490 BC, 480–479 BC) were to show, hoplites were extremely formidable.

Panoply

The hoplite panoply (*panoplia*) consisted of a round, soup bowl-shaped shield (*aspis*, Thucydides 7.82.3, Xenophon *Hellenika* 2.4.12, 5.4.18, cf. *hoplon*, Diodoros 15.44.3), approximately 90cm in diameter, a bronze helmet, a bronze or linen corselet and bronze greaves. The whole, when worn, weighed anywhere from 22.7 to 31.7kg.

Built on a wooden core, the shield was faced with a thin layer of stressed bronze and backed by leather. Because of its great weight, about 6.8 to 9.1kg, the shield was carried by an arrangement of two handles, the armband (*porpax*) in the centre through which the forearm passed and the handgrip (*antilabē*) at the rim. Held across the chest, it covered the hoplite from chin to knee. However, being clamped to the left arm it only offered protection to his left-hand side.

Above the flat broad rim of the shield, a hoplite's head was fully protected by a bronze helmet, the Corinthian helmet being by far the most common style. This was shaped from a single sheet of bronze that covered the entire face leaving only the eyes clear. Under the helmet many men either wore a cloth headband or an under-cap of felt, which not only restrained the hair but also provided some support for this heavy piece of armour. The stress on protection seriously impaired both hearing and vision, thus out of battle it could be pushed to the back of the head, thereby leaving the face uncovered.

A corslet protected the torso. This was either of bronze or of linen (*linothōrax*). The first, reaching a thickness of about 1.27cm, was a bell-shaped plate corslet composed of two sections fore-and-aft. The second was built up of multiple layers of linen glued together to form a stiff shirt, about half a centimetre thick. Below the waist it was cut into strips (*pteruges*, 'feathers') for ease of movement, with a second layer of *pteruges* being fixed behind the first, thereby covering the gaps between them. The great advantage of the *linothōrax* was its flexibility. Finally, a pair of bronze greaves (*knemides*) protected the lower legs. These clipped neatly round the calves by their own elasticity. Thus the hoplite remained effectively armoured from head-to-foot.

The weapon par excellence of the hoplite was the long-thrusting spear (*doru*), some 2.1 to 3m in length, made of ash and equipped with a bronze or iron spearhead and bronze butt-spike. The butt-spike, affectionately known as the 'lizard-sticker' (*sauroter*), allowed the spear to be planted upright in the ground when a hoplite was ordered to ground arms (being bronze it did not rust), or to fight with if his spear snapped in the mêlée. The spear was usually thrust over-arm, although it could be easily thrust under-arm if the hoplite was charging into contact at a run. Also carried was a short iron sword (*kopis*) with a heavy, leaf-shaped blade designed for slashing, but this was very much a secondary weapon.

Battle

Forget strategy and tactics, hoplite battle was, by its very nature, ritualistic – the idea was to defeat rather than to annihilate. The Greeks had developed what has been called by Hanson the 'Western way of War' – a head-to-head collision of summertime soldier-farmers on an open plain in a brutal display of courage and physical prowess. Their battlefields were scenes of furious fighting and carnage that usually consumed not more than an hour or two. Every man was pushed to the limits of his physical and psychological endurance – and then it was over, not to be repeated for a year or more.

That hoplites fought on the flattest piece of terrain was a point made by Mardonios in his speech to his master, Xerxes, the Great King of Persia (Herodotos 7.9β.1):

The Greeks are pugnacious enough, and start fights on the spur of the moment without sense or judgement to justify them. When they declare

war on each other, they go off together to the smoothest and flattest piece of ground they can find, and have their battle on it.

Although Mardonios believed that the Greeks pursued their unique style of warfare out of ignorance and stupidity, what he says is incontrovertible. For any unexpected obstacle could bring the phalanx to a complete halt or break its formation, and Aristotle (*Politics* 1303b16) reminds us that it would break up if it were forced to cross even the smallest watercourse. As a result generals (*stratēgoi*) selected level plains on which to fight their battles.

Once a *stratēgos* had deployed his hoplites and battle had been joined, there was little or no room for command or manoeuvre, the individual *stratēgos* taking up his position in the front rank of the phalanx and fighting alongside his men for the duration. Consequently, many *stratēgoi* perished in the fray. It was outward displays of grit (*aretē, andreía*), not strategic or tactical skills, which were all-important for a *stratēgos*.

Phalanx

It was the hoplite shield that made the rigid phalanx formation viable. Half the shield protruded beyond the left-hand side of the hoplite. If the man on the left moved in close he was protected by the shield overlap, which thus guarded his uncovered side. Hence, hoplites stood shoulder to shoulder with their shields locked. Once this formation was broken, however, the advantage of the shield was lost – as Plutarch says (*Moralia* 220A2), the armour of a hoplite may be for the individual's protection, but the hoplite's shield protected the whole phalanx. Thus the injunction of a Spartan mother to her son 'either with this or on this' (Plutarch *Moralia* 241F16), that is, he was to return home both alive and victorious carrying the shield, or lying dead upon it after a fight to the finish.

As the phalanx itself was the tactic, two opposing phalanxes would head straight for each other, break into a run for the last few metres, collide with a crash, and then stab and shove till one side broke. Thucydides famously says

ABOVE LEFT A Utopian philosopher, Plato had little sympathy with Athenian democracy. In his eyes, it was almost better to lose heroically on the hoplite battlefield than to win at sea or from behind city walls with the help of the *hoi polloí*. (Author's collection)

ABOVE RIGHT Aristotle believed that every living thing has built into it at conception its predestined final end, its perfect form. The 'end' of all human social life and organization was for the teleological philosopher the *polis*. (Author's collection)

An un-costly affair

Storming parties of 'barbarian' mercenaries were the exception that proves the rule, namely Greek states would shy away from heavy losses among their citizen-hoplites in what was the hazardous adventure of a head-on assault upon a fortified position.

In 413 BC 1,300 Thracian peltasts, known for their fighting skills and the use of the short sword, arrived in Athens too late to sail with the relief force headed for Syracuse (Thucydides 7.27.1). As the Athenians had no wish to incur unnecessary expenditure, they were sent back under the command of Diitrephes and 'as they were to sail through the Euripos, he was instructed to use them in doing whatever damage he could to the enemy on their voyage along the coastline' (Thucydides 7.29.1). First raiding Tanagra, these troops were then unleashed against Mykalessos, which was stormed one morning at daybreak.

Arguably these barbarians were expendable, but this small Boiotian town was clearly so far inland that the inhabitants never thought they would be attacked from the sea. Further, 'the fortifications were weak and had fallen down in places (it had been built in a hurry) and the gates were open because of the populace's false sense of security' (Thucydides 7.29.3). What followed was one of the worst atrocities of the Peloponnesian War. The Thracians 'butchered the inhabitants sparing neither the young nor the old, but methodically killing everyone they met, women and children alike, and even livestock and every living thing they saw' (Thucydides 7.29.4). Surprise was total and the lack of preparation by the defenders made it an easy target, as Thucydides, with controlled indignation, painfully records.

(5.71.1) that an advancing phalanx tended to crab to the right. The extreme right-hand man drifted in fear of being caught on his unshielded side, and the rest of the phalanx would naturally follow suit, each hoplite edging into the shadow of the shield of the comrade on his right. Thus each right wing might overlap and beat the opposing left.

A phalanx was a deep formation, normally composed of hoplites arrayed eight to 12 shields deep. In this dense mass only the front two ranks could use their spears in the mêlée, those in the third rank and beyond adding weight to the attack by pushing to their front. This was probably achieved by pressing the shield squarely into the hollow of the man in front's back, seating the left shoulder beneath the upper rim, and, digging the soles and toes into the ground for purchase, heaving. Both Thucydides (4.43.3, 96.2, cf. 6.70.2) and Xenophon (*Hellenika* 4.3.19, 6.4.14, cf. *Memorabilia* 3.1.18) commonly refer to the push and shove (*othismos*) of a hoplite mêlée. Once experienced such a thing was never easily forgotten and even Aristophanes' chorus of veteran hoplites is made to say (*Wasps* 1081–85):

> After running out with the spear and shield, we fought them ... each man stood up against each man ... we pushed them with the gods until evening

The pushing with the shields explains the famous cry of Epameinondas, who had introduced a 50-deep phalanx, 'for one pace more' at Leuktra (Polyainos 2.3.2, cf. 3.9.27, 4.3.8).

The mêlée itself was a toe-to-toe affair, the front two ranks of opposing phalanxes attempting to stab their spears into the exposed parts – throat, groin or thighs – of the enemy. Meantime, the ranks behind would thrust their shields flush against the backs of the men in file before them and shove with all their strength. Once a hoplite was down, injured or not, he was unlikely ever to get up again. This short but vicious 'scrum' was resolved once one side had practically collapsed. The phalanx became a mass, then a mob. There was no pursuit by the victors, and those of the vanquished who were able fled the battlefield.

Siegecraft

For most of the classical period fortification walls do not have a place in that central moment of Greek warfare, the clash of opposing phalanxes. The ethic of hoplite warfare and the practical restrictions imposed by the heavy panoply meant the hoplite was ill equipped to deal with the difficulties of cracking fortified positions. The equation between hoplite status and citizenship also made the rate of casualties a significant political consideration and the relatively small citizen populations of many of the *poleis* magnified this factor. Since the hazardous adventure of a direct assault generally imposed the greatest number of losses, there was a tendency to shun such operations unless unavoidable. Cities stated to have been taken by storm (*katà krátos*) were insignificant or un-walled (Thucydides 2.30.1 [Astakos], 3.97.2 [Aigition], 5.6.1 [Galepsos], 8.62.2 [Lampsakos], Diodoros 14.36.2-3 [Magnesia], Xenophon *Hellenika* 7.1.28 [Karyai], 4.20 [Kromnos]).

What the citizens of a *polis* had to fear most from their fellow Greeks was reduction by starvation or their betrayal to the enemy from within. Although Perikles is credited with the use of siege devices against Samos (Diodoros 12.28.3), the city held out for eight months and then capitulated (Thucydides 1.117.3), which suggests that it was reduced by blockade, by starvation or the fear of starvation, rather than by direct assault. Plataia, after ingenious attacks which seem to have been the acme of contemporary Greek siegecraft was, in the end, left to fall to the long-drawn pressure of starvation after two years of close-drawn circumvallation (Thucydides 2.75–78, 3.52.1–2). Actually this siege highlights the real weakness of Greek siegecraft, and is a clear indication of the difficulties that still stood in the way of capturing a fortified position during the Peloponnesian War even with the latest techniques available.

'New Model' phalanx

Macedon was a poor country on the northern rim of the Aegean, and the Macedonian phalanx was composed of peasant levies – all healthy male subjects of the king were liable for service – who could ill afford the panoply of a Greek hoplite. Consequently, they were issued, at state expense, with the *sarissa* and light body armour. As the new weapon required both hands for adequate control and handling, a button-shaped shield, some 60cm in diameter, was hung from the neck by means of a neck-strap and manoeuvred with the forearm as required (Polyainos 4.2.10, Asklepiodotus *Taktika* 5.1, Polybios 18.29.2).

The mobilization of the peasantry as a political tool, as well as a military force, may predate Philip if Anaximenes is heeded. He says it was Philip's eldest brother, Alexander II, who created and organized Macedon's first heavily armed infantry, and awarded them the honorific title of Foot-Companions (*pezhetairoi*) to enhance their prestige (Anaximenes *FGrHist* 72 F 4 = Harding 50B, cf. Demosthenes 2.17 with scholion = Harding 50A). But Alexander II only reigned for a year (370/369–369/368 BC) – a rival assassinated him. It is highly probable that the introduction of the 10 to 12-cubit (4.8–5.4m) *sarissa* as the principal offensive infantry weapon was Philip's innovation, particularly if in translation Anaximenes' text had been corrupted and thus should read 'Philip father of Alexander' and not 'Alexander'. That is certainly implied by Diodoros when he says Philip was 'the first to organize the Macedonian phalanx' (16.3.2, cf. Marsyas *FGrHist* 135 F 17).

Philip's first battle was against the Illyrians near lake Lychnitis (359/358 BC). Diodoros, drawing upon the mid-4th-century BC author Theopompos, states that Philip led the right wing, 'which consisted of the flower of the Macedonians' (16.4.5, cf. Theopompos *FGrHist* 115 F 348). It is assumed Diodoros is referring here to the *pezhetairoi*, Philip having 'ordered his cavalry (*hetairoi*) to ride past the barbarians and attack them on the flank, while he himself falling on the enemy in a frontal assault' (16.4.5). So, by leading them in person, Philip gave the newly established Macedonian phalanx a psychological boost.

The *sarissa* was made of a long shaft of cornel wood (*Cornus mas*, cornelian cherry), the shaft being of two-piece construction fitted together by a bronze coupling sleeve. Equipped with an iron leaf-shaped blade and bronze butt-spike – both about 50cm in length – and weighing around 6kg, the *sarissa* was held with a two-handed grip 1.8m from the butt. This meant the weapon extended some 3.6m in front of the Macedonian phalangite, thus giving him a reach of over 2.4m more than the Greek hoplite. In addition, the first five, not two ranks were now thrusting, giving 40 per cent more spearheads in the killing zone. Such a hedgehog-like front provided an unusual degree of offensive might, as well as defensive protection for the lightly armoured initial ranks. Under Philip the usual depth may have been 10 ranks, as a file was called a *dekás*. But to be tactically successful, the Macedonian phalanx needed a rank and file that was tough, disciplined and well trained. These requirements certainly tie in with Philip's regime to toughen up his troops by forced marches under arms and loaded down with rations and equipment (Diodoros 16.3.1, Polyainos 4.2.1, 2, 10, 15, Frontinus *Stratagems* 4.1.6). The use of tightly packed spearmen in the phalanx may have been a Greek development, but it reached its peak of efficiency and prowess in the Macedonian armies commanded by Philip and his son Alexander.

The Athenians had some reputation for siegecraft (Thucydides 1.102.2, cf. Herodotos 9.70.2–3, 102.1), but Potidaia held out against them for nearly three years and then surrendered only on terms, and that too although it was important for Athenian prestige to bring the siege to an end as quickly and decisively as possible (Thucydides 2.70.1–3, Diodoros 12.46.4–6). When Mytilene revolted against Athens the city could not be taken until the beginning of starvation led to its surrender. In fact capitulation only came about when the mass of the citizens were armed and were able to get their way against the more determined aristocrats who had been responsible for bringing about the rebellion in the first place (Thucydides 3.27–28). Likewise, some form of *coup de main*, helped by local treachery, captured the Long Walls at Megara (Thucydides 4.66–68).

For the Athenians the prolonged encirclement and starvation of the trapped populace may have been the keys to victory, but mounting a formal siege was a ruinously expensive undertaking. The siege of Samos had cost over 1,400 talents (*IG* i³ 363.19 = Fornara 113, cf. Plutarch *Perikles* 28.1), while that of Potidaia was an even greater financial drain, costing no less than 2,000 talents or two-fifths of the reserves of Athens (Thucydides 2.70.2, cf. Diodoros 12.46.4). But it was the siege of Mytilene that strained Athenian fiscal resources almost to breaking point. The Athenians, needing money for the siege, decided on a desperate solution and 'raised among themselves for the first time a property tax of 200 talents' (Thucydides 3.19.1, cf. 1.141.5).

During the latter half of the 5th century BC, the Greeks certainly used siege-mounds and deployed 'machines' (*mēchanai*). This unqualified term is entirely indefinite, but almost certainly included the scaling-ladder, battering ram, tortoise and shed, although not the catapult. The absence of artillery from the detailed military narrative of Thucydides is one of the strongest arguments for thinking that it had not been invented before the turn of the 4th century BC.

Engines of war

Samos	440 BC	Plutarch *Perikles* 27 Diodoros 12.28.3	*Mēchanai* Battering rams (*krioùs*), tortoises (*chelōnas*)
Oinoe	431 BC	Thucydides 2.18.1	*Mēchanai*, possibly battering rams
Potidaia	430 BC	Thucydides 2.58.1 Diodoros 12.46.2	*Mēchanai* *Mēchanai*, possibly battering rams, tortoises
Plataia	430/429 BC	Thucydides 2.76.4	Battering rams (*mēchanai*)
Minoa	427 BC	Thucydides 3.51.3	*Mēchanai*, possibly scaling-ladders
Pylos	425 BC	Thucydides 4.13.1	*Mēchanai*, possibly scaling-ladders
Peiraieus	403 BC	Xenophon *Hellenika* 2.4.27	*Mēchanopoios*, possibly battering rams

The non-torsion catapult was first deployed, in the form of a simple 'belly-shooter' (*gastraphetes*), by Dionysios I of Syracuse during his siege of Motya, the Carthaginian island-fortress at the west end of Sicily, in 398/397 BC (Diodoros 14.50.4, cf. 41.4). In essence an over-large crossbow, it acquired this seemingly homely and unthreatening name because a concavity at the rear of the wooden stock was placed against the stomach and the weight of the body was used to force back the bowstring to its maximum extension (Heron *Belopoiika* 81). The revolutionary development of this mechanical propulsive device, which essentially accumulated and stored human strength, would eventually threaten fortifications by the sheer amount of force it could produce. Catapults would come to epitomize the acme of ancient military technology.

But in the first half of the 4th century BC the full effect of siege-machines was yet to be realized. In his treatise *Poliorkētika* (or *How to Survive under Siege*), the Arcadian soldier-of-fortune Aineias Taktikos (*fl.* 350 BC) writes from the point of view of personal experience. Despite the beginnings of the mechanization of siegecraft – and here the techniques of defence he discusses are almost wholly non-mechanical, mentioning artillery only once (32.8) – the major preoccupation of Aineias remains the threat of betrayal (1.3–7, 11.1–2).

The double-gripped, concave hoplite shield, seen here on the Nereid monument, was singular. Greek phalanxes were calibrated by the depth of their cumulative shields – 'eight shields deep', 'twelve shields deep' – not by counting spears. (Author's collection)

The sites at war

Siege of Plataia (429–427 BC)

The Spartans, led by Archidamos II, and their Peloponnesian and Boiotian allies laid siege to Athens' oldest ally Plataia, a small Boiotian *polis* at the north foot of Mount Kithairon (summer 429 BC). Assurances from the Athenians that they would not abandon the Plataians 'but would aid them with all their power' (Thucydides 2.73.3) convinced those still inside the city walls to hold out.

Initially, the besiegers erected a surrounding palisade to keep any defenders from escaping. Next they began building a siege-mound, using local timber to form a latticework, which was then packed with earth and stone. As the siege-mound neared the defences, the besieged responded by erecting a wooden scaffold, and inside this men raised the wall facing the growing ramp by using bricks procured from nearby houses. The timbers were covered in rawhide, 'so that the workmen and woodwork might be safe and shielded from incendiary arrows' (Thucydides 2.75.5).

Once the siege-mound reached the wall, a feat taking 70 days and nights, the Plataians tunnelled through and attempted to undermine it. The besiegers countered by using reed wattles packed with clay to provide a tough facing to the ramp. They then deployed battering rams against the raised wall but the Plataians responded by lowering nooses and hoisting up the rams. They also used cranes to drop heavy beams on the rams so as to snap their heads off. Despite these countermeasures, however, sections of the raised wall collapsed under the battering. Wisely the defenders had earlier constructed a second semicircular wall within the city (a lunette), so that when the attackers broke in they found themselves in a walled enclosure.

In reply the besiegers filled the enclosure with bundles of wood and fired them using liberal quantities of pine resin and in a bold innovation, sulphur. The combination of sulphur and pitch 'produced such a conflagration as had never been seen before, greater than any fire produced by human agency' (Thucydides 2.77.4). This chemically enhanced fire almost destroyed the Plataians for, along with the bright blue sulphur flames and the acrid stench, the fumes would have been deadly since the combustion of sulphur creates sulphur dioxide. A chance rainstorm, however, doused this toxic conflagration. After this final failure, Archidamos sent many of his troops home to attend the harvest, while having the remainder build a double wall of circumvallation with a view to starving the Plataians into submission (autumn 429 BC). Some 2,000 Spartan and Boiotian troops remained on guard duty through the winter.

Most of the Plataians had escaped before the siege began and only a garrison of 480 men, 80 of them Athenian, and 110 women 'to make bread' (Thucydides 2.78.3) remained in the beleaguered city. The small garrison and wise stockpiling of provisions meant that the defenders were in no immediate danger of starvation. In fact they held out for two years. Half the garrison managed to escape in the last months of the siege by negotiating the circumvallation one stormy, moonless night in midwinter, and then eluding a large pursuing force, but the remainder held out in the pathetic belief that the Athenians would relieve them. In the end, facing starvation, they surrendered (summer 427 BC). Under pressure from Thebes, Plataia's hereditary enemy, and after some specious legal proceedings, the Spartans executed all 225 male survivors, which included some 25 Athenians, and sold the women into slavery. They then turned Plataia over to the Thebans, who levelled the city entirely (Thucydides 3.20–24, 52–68).

The Peloponnesian siege-mound at Plataia (summer 429 BC)

For 70 days and nights continuously the Peloponnesians kept on raising the siege-mound. First, containing walls of timber laid like latticework were constructed to contain the mound. Next, the spaces between the timber walls were filled with earth, rubble and wood. Naturally, the mound builders required some form of protection that would permit them to work unhindered. The solution was a shed, a light timber structure open-ended with wickerwork sides, a boarded roof and a fireproof covering of rawhide. Several of these were arranged end-to-end to form a corridor. The Plataians countered by heightening the fortifications with a wooden framework within which they erected a wall using bricks from the nearest houses. The structure was covered with hides to protect the workmen and to prevent incendiary devices reaching the woodwork.

The Athenian siege of Syracuse (summer 414 BC)

The Athenians took up a position on the dominating heights, called Epipolai, north of Syracuse. There they built two forts, the Labdalum and 'the Circle'. From the latter they began to construct a double line of ditches and palisades from sea to sea in order to blockade the city. The Syracusans tried to prevent them with counter-walls, each a combination of ditch and palisade, at X–X, Y–Y, and finally succeeded with Z–Z after capturing the fort at Labdalum. The latter wall ran west from the city and cut across Epipolai, thereby precluding the Athenian attempt to reach the sea at Trogilos and isolate the city. With the loss of Labdalum, the Athenians fortified a key piece of terrain – Plemmyrion – near the mouth of the Great Harbour in order to ensure access control for supplies.

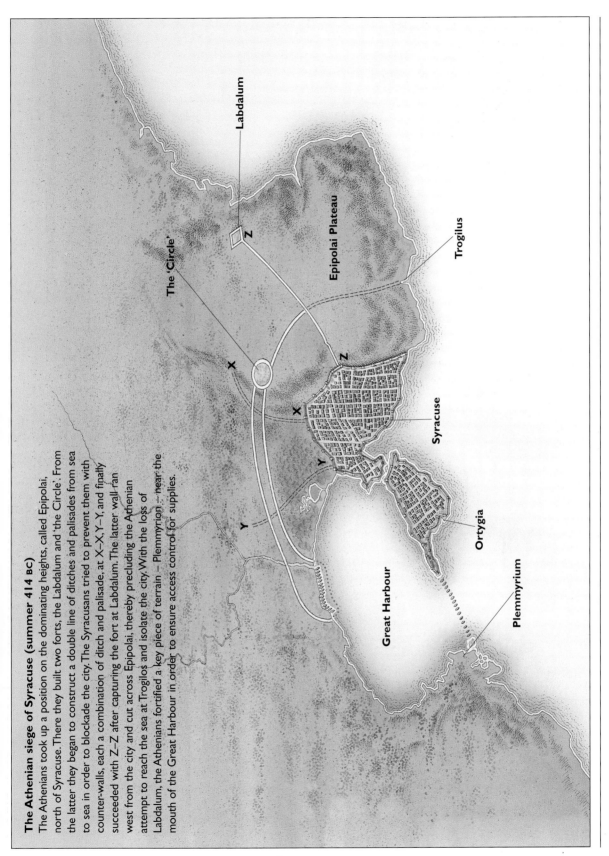

Labdalum

The 'Circle'

Epipolai Plateau

Trogilus

Syracuse

Ortygia

Great Harbour

Plemmyrium

Siege of Syracuse (415–413 BC)

In 415 BC, with the Peloponnesian War in a state of uneasy truce, Athens, ostensibly to preserve the independence of her allies Egesta and Leontini, launched an expedition under Nikias, Lamachos and Alkibiades to capture Syracuse. From the outset the Athenians suffered from command problems. Alkibiades, summoned home to answer a charge of sacrilege, deserted to Sparta, and the able Lamachos was killed during the early stages of the siege. This left Nikias, whom Thucydides (7.42.3, cf. 2.65.11) represents as timid, incompetent and notoriously superstitious, in command. The armada included 134 fighting triremes, 60 of them Athenian, and an unknown number of troopships carrying 5,100 hoplites, 1,500 of them Athenian, with light-armed troops, including archers from Crete and slingers from Rhodes, in proportion. Athens also supplied 700 *thētes*, who normally shipped as citizen-oarsmen, equipped as hoplites so as to serve as marines (*epibatai*) on the triremes (Thucydides 6.43, cf. 8.2, IG i³ 93.6 = Fornara 146).

The Athenians severed Syracuse's land communications with two forts. One was planted at Syce north-west of the city and not far from the southern edge of the rocky heights, called Epipolai, overlooking the city. The other fort was placed at Labdalum on Epipolai's northern escarpment line. Thucydides calls the fort at Syce 'the Circle' (6.98.2) and this was to be the centre of operations for the Athenians while they conducted the siege. At their other fort, that at Labdalum, the Athenians stored their supplies, equipment and war-chest. They also began to construct a double wall of circumvallation from 'the Circle', northwards in the direction of Trogilos and southwards towards the Great Harbour. The Athenians, however, left their northern walls, those running across Epipolai to the sea at Trogilos, incomplete, which was to prove disastrous. Meanwhile the fleet prepared to blockade Syracuse by sea. After two attempts to build counter-walls (*hypoteichisma*) from their defences were defeated, the Syracusans were then dismayed to see the Athenian fleet sailing into their Great Harbour.

The Syracusans had sent urgent messages to the Peloponnese asking for assistance and Corinth, as the *metropolis* of Syracuse, had pressed Sparta to act. Corinth and Sparta despatched only a few triremes and a handful of troops, but the Spartans supplied a determined and resourceful *stratēgos*, Gylippos (Thucydides 6.93.2). He slipped past Nikias and entered the city. There he put fresh heart into the beleaguered Syracusans, who captured the fort at Labdalum and the unfinished northern fortifications on Epipolai and started the construction of four fortified camps and a third counter-wall, which was to run north of 'the Circle' parallel to Epipolai's northern escarpment line. The Syracusans' confidence increased dramatically, so much so that they began to train their naval crews with the intention of challenging the Athenian fleet.

Nikias now saw the danger of the besiegers being besieged and wrote to Athens to ask permission to retire or, failing that, for more troops to be sent (summer 414 BC). The assembly voted for a second expedition. Before it arrived, however, the Syracusans managed to seize the three forts – the supply depot built to replace Labdalum – at Plemmyrion, a promontory forming the southern side of the narrow entrance to the Great Harbour. This victory demonstrated once and for all that the Athenians could be defeated with the right combination of land and naval forces. To overcome their vulnerability on the sea, the Syracusans had cut down the bows of their triremes and reinforced them with stay-beams so that they could ram head-on instead of from the flank or stern as the skilled Athenians preferred: their sleek triremes were fast and manoeuvrable, the epitome of efficient muscle power.

This defeat forced the Athenians to crowd into an inadequate camp in unhealthy, marshy ground on the west side of the Great Harbour (spring 413 BC). But the strategic cost of the capture of Plemmyrion was even greater as the Syracusans now held both sides of the harbour. The Athenians could no longer bring in supplies, and 'the loss of Plemmyrion brought bewilderment and discouragement to the army' (Thucydides 7.24.3).

Just as things were looking bleak for Nikias and his men, however, Demosthenes, the leader of the second expedition, sailed into the Great Harbour with 73 triremes carrying almost 5,000 hoplites, and swarms of light-armed troops 'both from Greece and from outside' (Thucydides 7.42.1). With his characteristic clarity and boldness Demosthenes recommended a night attack to destroy the Syracusans' counter-wall and seize Epipolai, for without the heights no assault on the city could prevail. But this ended in confusion and failure, 'a great many of the Athenians and allies were killed, although still more arms were taken than could be accounted for by the number of the dead' (Thucydides 7.45).

Demosthenes realized evacuation was the only way to save the Athenian force, but a lunar eclipse caused the superstitious Nikias to delay the expedition's departure for 'thrice nine' days. The Syracusans discovered the Athenian plan to retire and thus became more determined than ever not to relax their pressure and to force the enemy to fight again in the confined space of the Great Harbour. Defeated at sea, the Athenians resolved to try to break through the improvised boom of merchantmen thrown across the harbour mouth by the Syracusans, but their ships were driven into the centre of the harbour and attacked. After a daylong struggle – the Athenians had strengthened the bows of their triremes in the Syracusan manner and boarded everyone likely to be of service as a marine – the Athenians fell back on their camp.

Abandoning their sick and wounded, the Athenian army of 40,000 men now attempted to withdraw overland to reach friendly Katana. Nikias led the van while Demosthenes commanded the rearguard, but the two columns became separated under the constant harrying of the Syracusan horsemen and light-armed troops. Demosthenes' force was trapped, 20,000 men were killed and some 6,000 surrendered. Meanwhile Nikias' starved and thirsty force had made its way to the Assinaros and, while slacking their thirst, was attacked by the Syracusans, who slaughtered them as they drank from the river, 'all muddy as it was and stained with blood' (Thucydides 7.84.4). Nikias surrendered himself to stop the slaughter and the few survivors were taken prisoner.

Both *stratēgoi* were executed without trial (Thucydides 7.86.2). The prisoners were sent to the quarries, where all perished of exposure, starvation or disease after 70 days of incarceration there, save for the few who were lucky enough to be sold into slavery or those who, according to legend, were able to recite verses by Euripides from memory (Plutarch *Nikias* 29.2). This was Athens' greatest reverse and a turning point in the war. Thucydides, emphasizing the foolhardy ambition so typical of imperial democracy, says, 'the Athenians were beaten at all areas and altogether; all they suffered was great; they were annihilated, as the saying goes, with a total annihilation, their fleet, their army – everything was annihilated, and few out of many returned home' (7.87.6).

Siege of Mantineia (385 BC)

Interfering with water by diverting rivers was an environmental ploy that was capable of wreaking great havoc. Pausanias, in his description (8.8.7–8, cf. Apollodoros *Poliorkētika* 157.1–158.3) of the siege of Mantineia mounted by Agesipolis of Sparta, pinpoints the mechanical strength of mud-brick fortifications:

Against the blows of engines brick brings greater security than fortifications built of stone. For stones break and are dislodged from their fittings; brick however, does not suffer so much from engines, but it crumbles under the action of water just as wax is melted by the sun.

Then again, Agesipolis' conquest of Mantineia also highlights the structural weakness of brickwork and the destructive potential of water.

LEFT The epic siege was prominent in the Greeks' view of their early history, namely the ten-year siege of Troy. Despite this, Greece lagged behind the Near East in the development of siegecraft. Seen here is the Persian siege-mound at Palaipaphos. (Author's collection)

BELOW The North-East Gate of Palaipaphos, seen here from the inner gate, formed one of the strongholds of the fortifications. The thoroughfare into the city led through a narrow passage with a sharp double bend, which was overlooked by two massive bastions. (Author's collection)

The Persian siege of Palaipaphos (498 BC)

Effective tactics and techniques for siege warfare were developed by large territorial Near-Eastern monarchies that possessed and were able to mobilize the necessary resources. Of these the use of siege-mounds was the simplest, and promised the quickest results if conditions were ideal. The Assyrians employed them with ruthless skill, as did the Lydians and Persians. Herodotos says (1.16.2) Alyattes of Lydia took Smyrna (c.600 BC), and the discovery there of a huge ramp of earth and felled trees, as well as stones, mud-bricks and timbers from nearby houses, strongly suggests that this was the method by which the Lydians stormed the Greek city. According to archaeological evidence, the ensuing action was essentially one fought with long-range weapons; some 125 bronze arrowheads both leaf-shape and of the triangular 'Scythian' form, peppered the city and the siege-mound itself (Cook 1958–59: 24). A century on, the Persians under Harpagos easily carried the Ionian cities by direct assault, using the siege-mound to get men up and over the enemy walls (Herodotos 1.162.2).

Having described in great detail the double battle of Salamis, Herodotos then glosses over the Persian re-conquest of Cyprus (498/497 BC). He says, 'of the besieged cities, Soli held out the longest; it fell in the fifth month after the Persians had undermined its walls' (5.115.2). One of the anonymous 'besieged cities' was Palaipaphos (Kouklia) and the siege-mound erected by the Persians has been identified. Located near the North-East Gate, excavations in and around the siege-mound have revealed the buried remains of elaborate siege and counter-siege works. The siege-mound was constructed out of the wreckage from a nearby sanctuary, together with earth and timber to fill the fosse and raise a 7m-high ramp against the defences. Finds included some 500 bronze and iron arrowheads and spearheads, and a Corinthian helmet dated to around 500 BC, which represents the only hoplite helmet found so far in a battle context.

The distribution of missiles through the siege-mound reveals the tactics of both sides. Three-winged arrowheads of an eastern type, made to a standard pattern, were concentrated in particular areas of the siege-mound, notably in the re-entrant between the curtain-wall and north-western bastion of the North-East Gate. These were the standardized weapons of professional archers, who provided covering fire during the operation and concentrated firepower for the final assault. In contrast, four-sided javelin heads, crudely made, were scattered widely over

the siege-mound. They obviously belonged to the defence, able with the advantage of height to hurl javelins in a pattern of continual harassment. Stone balls of varying weight from 2.7 to 21.8kg were found not concentrated, but scattered mainly along the base of the fortifications. They probably belong to the defence rather than the attack, and represent attempts to crush the attackers in the final, desperate stage of the siege – heads would have offered no more resistance than rotten apples to

these descending stones. The impression is on the attacking side of a thoroughly professional body with a well-established technique of siegecraft, which relied not on artillery (yet to be invented) to take the city but on the siege-mound, built doubtless by impressed local labour and protected by Persian archery.

Nevertheless, it appears the Persians did not gain Palaipaphos without a fierce struggle for the siege-mound had been undermined by the besieged in two different ways. First, by a passage dug through the berm and, second, by four tunnels cut through the bedrock underneath the fortifications, the wooden pit props of Tunnels 1 and 3 having been fired on completion by means of some flammable substance (possibly sulphur and pitch) carried in large bronze cauldrons.

ABOVE LEFT Four rock-hewn tunnels passing beneath the walls of Palaipaphos undermined the Persian siege-mound. Tunnel 1, seen here, was dug 2.8m below the base of the circuit and continued through the soft conglomerate rock until it reached the bottom of the fosse. (Author's collection)

ABOVE RIGHT Through Tunnel 1 as much material of the Persian ramp as possible was removed, and the cavity propped up with timber. By means of some flammable substance carried in a large bronze cauldron – note here calcined stone – the timbers were burnt. (Author's collection)

The bas-reliefs from the Nereid monument are notable for their depiction of a siege in operation. Although a non-Greek dynast, the commissioner was obviously in close contact with Greek culture and society, as the scenes represented on his tomb were purely Hellenic. (Author's collection)

'Ask me for an image of civilization', said Seneca, 'and I'll show you the sack of a great city'. In this scene from the Nereid monument hoplites armed with stones, man the battlements. In the middle of the city is a woman. She alone looks out of the sculpture straight at the viewer. (Author's collection)

After laying waste to the surrounding countryside, Agesipolis detailed half his troops to dig a trench and erect a palisade around Mantineia, thereby investing it. The Mantineians, however, opted to resist as they had taken the precaution of stockpiling a large reserve of grain within their city walls. Not wishing to commit his Peloponnesian allies to a long and drawn-out siege, Agesipolis decided to mount an aquatic attack against Mantineia. This was accomplished by diverting the Ophis, the river that flowed through the city, by means of a makeshift dam. The heavy rains of the previous winter meant that the river was in full spate, and the diverted water rapidly rose above the stone socle of the circuit. As the rising water begun to affect the lower courses of mud-brick, the upper ones also weakened. At first cracks appeared in the brickwork and then signs of collapse.

Despite the Mantineians valiantly shoring up their crumbling defences with timber baulks, total collapse was imminent, and so it was decided that the best course of action was to surrender the city to Agesipolis. He razed most of Mantineia to the ground and dispersed the Mantineians back to their ancestral villages (Xenophon *Hellenika* 5.2.4–5, cf. Diodoros 15.12.1).

Curiously Pausanias (8.8.9), in his version of the siege, concludes with the following statement:

Agesipolis did not discover this method of demolishing the fortifications of the Mantineians. It was a stratagem invented at an earlier date by Kimon, the son of Miltiades, when he was besieging Boges and other Persians who were holding Eïon on the Strymon.

However, although Herodotos (7.107.1), Thucydides (1.98.1), Plutarch (*Kimon* 7), Polyainos (7.24) and the *Oxrhynchus Papyri* (13.1610 F 6 = Fornara 61B2) all cite Kimon's attack on Eïon (477/476 BC), none of them mention that he flooded the city by damming up the Strymon. The capture of Eïon was celebrated in verse on three herms in Athens and the inscriptions, quoted by Aischines (3.183–85) and Plutarch (*Kimon* 7.3), support the above sources. But the diversion of the river, the cunning trick ascribed to Kimon by Pausanias, is probably a later invention to explain these 'Eïon epigrams'.

Following the defeat of the Spartans at Leuktra by Epameinondas, the Mantineians were able to re-establish their city (Xenophon *Hellenika* 6.5.3). Although still employing mud-brick in the construction of their new city walls, the Mantineians took the wise precaution of altering the channel of the Ophis so that it now flowed around, instead of through the city.

The sites today

The best location to survey the city walls of Athens is in the Kerameikós archaeological site (fenced), just 1km from Monastiráki (Metró, Line 1) via Odhós Ermoú. Here part of the City Wall runs for some 183m in a north–south direction and is interrupted by the Sacred Gate and the Dipylon Gate. The site also has a museum (Oberländer Museum) that holds, amongst other artefacts, the statues and stelai recovered from the Themistoklean circuit.

Much of the Long Walls have long disappeared. The northern wall follows the line of Odhós Piraiós and has been buried beneath the road. The southern wall is largely on the route of the original Athens–Peiraieus Electric Railway (Metró, Line 1). Sections of it can be seen in Néo Fáliro, and also on the seaward side of the line between Kallithéa and Moskháto stations.

Down in the Peiraieus a stretch of the Themistoklean circuit can be seen next to the Naval Museum of Greece, which is in the bay south of Zéa. By following the road (Aktí Themistokléous) just beyond the museum that runs round the Aktí peninsula, well-preserved stretches of the Kononian circuit can be seen edging the shore.

Gyphtokastro is on the old Athens–Thebes road, and its impressive remains still dominate the Káza pass between Attica and Boiotia. From the restaurant in Káza follow the gravel track signed Ancient Fortress of Eleutherae (open site).

Mantineia lies 12.5km north of Tripolis just off the Tripolis–Pirgos road (follow sign for Ancient Mantineia). The site itself (fenced but open) is opposite a bizarre church (1972), a Minoan-classical-Byzantine folly dedicated to Ayía Photeini.

Ancient Messene is just outside the village of Mavromáti, on the slopes of Mount Ithome. Just 1km to the north-west of the village are the impressive remains of the Arcadian Gate (still in use) and part of the city walls (open site). Most of the vast circuit has been unearthed or traced, and excavations at the archaeological site (fenced) at the southern edge of the village are ongoing.

Useful contact information

Oberländer Museum, Kerameikós
Tel.   (+30) 210 346 3552

Archaeological Museum, Messene
Tel.   (+30) 272 405 1201

Greek National Tourist Organization (EOT)
Tel.   (+30) 210 870 7000
Email   info@gnto.gr

Websites

Greek National Tourist Organization (EOT)
www.gnto.gr

Ministry of Culture
www.culture.gr

Hellenic Travelling (journal)
www.travelling@travelling.gr

Bibliography

Camp, J. M., 'Notes on the towers and borders of classical Boiotia', *American Journal of Archaeology* 95, 1991: 193–202

Camp, J. M., *The Archaeology of Athens*, London: Yale University Press, 2001

Cook, J. M., 'Old Smyrna, 1948–1951', *The Annual of the British School at Athens* 53–54, 1958–59: 1–34

Cooper, F. A., 'Epaminondas and Greek fortifications', *American Journal of Archaeology* 90, 1986: 195

Coulton, J. J., *Ancient Greek Architects at Work: Problems of Structure and Design*, Oxford: Oxbow Books, 1995

Harding, P., 'Athenian defensive strategy in the fourth century', *Phoenix* 42, 1988: 61–71

Kern, P. B., *Ancient Siege Warfare*, Bloomington: Indiana University Press, 1999

Knigge, U., *The Athenian Kerameikos: History – Monuments – Excavations*, Athens: Deutsches Archäologisches Institut Athen, 1991

Landels, J. G., *Engineering in the Ancient World*, London: Constable, 2000

Lawrence, A. W., *Greek Aims in Fortification*, Oxford: Oxford University Press, 1979

Lawrence, A. W. (revised by R.A. Tomlinson), *Greek Architecture*, London: Yale University Press, 1996

Marsden, E. W., *Greek and Roman Artillery: Historical Development*, Oxford: Oxford University Press, 1969, 1999

Munn, M., *The Defense of Attica*, Berkeley: University of California Press, 1993

Ober, J., *Fortress Attica: Defense of the Athenian Land Frontier, 404–322 BC*, Leiden: E.J. Brill, 1985

Ober, J., 'Early artillery towers: Messenia, Boiotia, Attica, Megarid', *American Journal of Archaeology* 91, 1987: 569–604

Ober, J., 'Defense of the Athenian Land Frontier, 404–322 BC: a reply', *Phoenix* 43, 1989: 294–301

Ober, J., 'Hoplites and obstacles', in V.D. Hanson (ed.) *Hoplites: The Classical Greek Battle Experience*, London: Routledge, 1991, 173–96

Ruschenbusch, E., 'Die Bevölkerungszahl Griechenlands im 5. und 4. Jhs', *Zeitschrift für Papyrologie und Epigraphik* 56, 1984: 55–57

Ruschenbusch, E., 'Normalpolis', *Zeitschrift für Papyrologie und Epigraphik* 59, 1985: 253–63

Sekunda, N. V., 'The *sarissa*', *Acta Universitatis Lodziensis* 23, 2001: 13–41

Scranton, R. L., *Greek Walls*, Cambridge, Mass.: Harvard University Press, 1941

Vanderpool, E., 'Roads and forts in northwestern Attica', *California Studies in Classical Antiquity* 11, 1978: 227–45

Westlake, H. D., 'The progress of *epiteichimos*'. *Classical Quarterly* 33, 1983: 12–24

Winter, F. E., *Greek Fortifications*, London: Routledge & Kegan Paul, 1971

Wycherley, R. E., *How Greeks Built Cities*, London: Norton, 1976

Glossary

Acropolis	Literally 'high city', the original citadel of a city
Chōra	Territory, often as opposed to the *polis* that exploited it
Cubit	Unit of measurement equal to the length from the elbow to the tip of the middle finger (= 462.4mm/18.21in.)
Deme	Athens was divided into 139 administrative districts or *demes*, many of which were within the city itself, but others were separate settlements scattered throughout the Attic countryside
Drachma	Silver coin, average daily wage of casual labourer
Drafted	Stone block with a chisel-dressed band round the edges as a guide for the levelling of the rest of the surface
Isodomic	Masonry set in courses of equal height
Mina/minae	Unit of weight equivalent to 100 Attic drachmas or 70 Aiginetan drachmas
Orthostate	Block set on edge, usually at the foot of a wall
Palisade	Barrier constructed from wooden stakes, which are positioned vertically in the ground
Parodos/parodoi	Wall-walk usually protected by a crenellated parapet
Polis/poleis	A *polis* in size was like a city but in its independence a state, politically, however, its citizens followed constitutional law and fought on the approval of the assembly
Poros	Soft coarse conchiferous limestone (tufa)
Postern	Also known as a sallyport, this was essentially not an entrance but an exit designed for sudden sortie and counter-attack
Talent	Fixed weight of silver equivalent to 60 *minae* (Attic-Euboic *tálanton* = 26.2kg, Aiginetan *tálanton* = 43.6kg)

Index

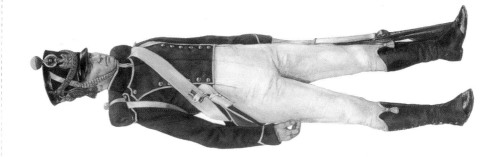

OSPREY
PUBLISHING

FIND OUT MORE ABOUT OSPREY

❏ Please send me the latest listing of Osprey's publications

❏ I would like to subscribe to Osprey's e-mail newsletter

Title / rank

Name

Address

City / county

Postcode / zip   state / country

e-mail

FOR

I am interested in:

❏ Ancient world   ❏ American Civil War
❏ Medieval world   ❏ World War 1
❏ 16th century   ❏ World War 2
❏ 17th century   ❏ Modern warfare
❏ 18th century   ❏ Military aviation
❏ Napoleonic   ❏ Naval warfare
❏ 19th century

Please send to:

North America:
Osprey Direct, c/o Random House Distribution Center,
400 Hahn Road, Westminster, MD 21157, USA

UK, Europe and rest of world:
Osprey Direct UK, P.O. Box 140, Wellingborough,
Northants, NN8 2FA, United Kingdom

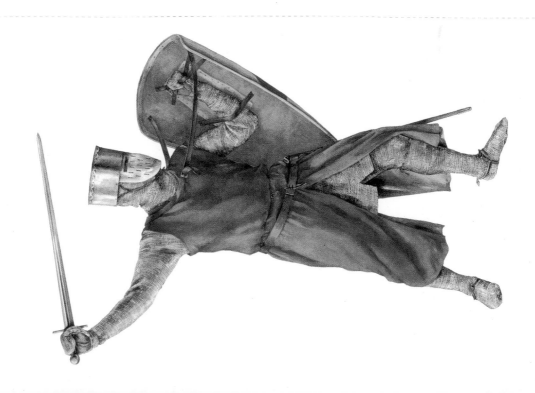

Young Guardsman
Figure taken from *Warrior 22:*
Imperial Guardsman 1799–1815
Published by Osprey
Illustrated by Richard Hook

www.ospreypublishing.com

OSPREY
PUBLISHING

Knight, c.1190
Figure taken from *Warrior 1: Norman Knight 950 – 1204 AD*
Published by Osprey
Illustrated by Christa Hook

POSTCARD

www.ospreypublishing.com